the vacant pulpit

JACK GILCHRIST

the vacant pulpit

THE JUDSON PRESS, Valley Forge

THE VACANT PULPIT

The Judson Press
Valley Forge, Pa. 19481

The author has used pseudonyms for all persons mentioned in this book and masked all geographical locations of churches in order to prevent any possible embarrassment to those who had a part in the events described in this book.

Standard Book No. 8170-0449-1
Library of Congress Catalog Card No. 77-81443

Printed in the U.S.A.

foreword

TWO-THIRDS OF THE WORTH of a book the author can provide — if he knows what he is writing about, and if he knows how to write about it. Jack Gilchrist knows both.

For several months he was more than "chairman" of the pulpit committee; he was its player-coach. And to the retelling of the encounters of his team he brought the successful experience of having published numerous articles and short stories. This intelligent and devoted layman is the executive of a considerable corporate business enterprise, and one suspects that as he fulfilled the successive growth steps to this position, his earlier bosses never found his written reports dull reading!

Locating, visiting, and evaluating prospects for the pastorate of a church of several hundred members, of whom more than an ordinary number are themselves very able people responsibly involved in the community and world mission of the church, is a business as significant as any industrial or commercial enterprise. Many of the qualities necessary for the one befit the other. This author clearly invested his talents as a faithful steward and will inspire lay readers to do likewise in similar circumstances. He is aware of the gospel; and he knows the world that needs it.

The third indispensable ingredient of a good book, of course, is the experience, interest, or perhaps specific need brought to the book by the reader himself. This account of the planning, travels, responses, and decisions of a pulpit committee will be enjoyable, frequently amusing, sometimes saddening, and most certainly helpful to many groups of people, in churches that call their own ministers, or take part in appointing them.

Most obviously, the book will help those now facing the responsibility of calling a minister themselves, and it will evoke empathetic response from any who have ever had the experience. The likely issues come up and are met decisively. The feelings of hope, exhilaration, discouragement, fresh discovery, and final satisfaction come through. Neither the author nor his committee would boast of their experience as a model without flaw. It will be, nevertheless, a guide in which the sound procedures and avoidable errors will be clear.

Not least interested will be pastors themselves who may learn here for the first time what searching scrutiny, what conjecture, or what demythologizing of credentials in their own candidacies may have been occasioned by the chance non-recurring particulars of a single sermon or a brief interview interposed between already pressing pastoral duties. They may come to have a new appreciation of the values, the seriousness, and the faith of lay leaders whose fellow members have placed upon them this formidable task.

Although the author and his church are American

Baptist, the story told here will correspond closely to the experience of the churches of several denominations of similar polity. The leaders of all such communions may be stimulated to reflect more deeply upon the pastoral placement procedures their churches practice and upon the yearning of honest, competent lay people for effective pastoral leadership.

HAROLD W. RICHARDSON

May 1, 1969

one

THE PHONE RANG. It rang again. No one moved to answer it. In the house was laughter and good cheer. It was a warm summer's night, a relaxed, peaceful evening that was easy to live.

But the phone rang again, not to be put off. And its ringing signaled a message that was to wipe out the laughter and put a chill on the summer evening breeze.

Lifting the receiver stopped the ringing. It also allowed the voice, the flat, bewildered voice, to give its message. The words were said strangely, mechanically, almost recited.

"Doctor Post has suffered a heart attack this evening. It proved fatal." What a way to talk! "Doctor Post had a heart attack this evening. It proved to be fatal." He's dead! Why don't they say he's dead?

People live and people die. When a man passes the age of sixty with steel gray hair and a lined face – when he walks with a stoop and a trace of weariness shows around the eyes – it is not unusual for death to call.

A man returned home with his wife after eating out and sat down in his easy chair to read the evening paper.

She carried on a conversation with him from the kitchen in the easy familiarity of thirty-odd years of marriage. His voice became inaudible. There was a gasp. She hurried into the living room. It was already too late. He was gone.

It is sad, for he was a good man. The bereaved – his wife, the family – will receive the sympathy and condolences of friends in proper fashion and time. But this was no ordinary man! He belonged not to a wife or family. He belonged to those whom he had baptized, married, counseled, and comforted. He belonged to the flock six hundred strong – well, perhaps not strong – six hundred lives that need, depend on the guidance, chiding, and encouragement of a gentle, yet firm shepherd.

The telephones rang on a warm August evening all across the city and in the suburbs beyond, bringing sorrow into the lives of the members of the First Baptist Church of Cedar City.

The First Baptist Church of Cedar City is located in the very heart of town and has been there for one hundred and twenty-seven years. Next door is the city hall. Across the street is the *Citizen Herald,* the local newspaper, and one block north is the busiest intersection in town. As the oldest and one of the most centrally located churches, the First Baptist Church required a pastor who was cosmopolitan in his ministry.

Dr. Frank Post was that. He had a ready and warm smile. A good listener, he spoke slowly, almost hesitantly, as though unwilling to interject his thoughts on the matter at hand. Yet, when he spoke, his voice had that ring of authority and assurance that caused people to listen.

Strangers from the street walked into his office for consultation and pastoral advice. The courts and law enforcement bureaus called him repeatedly for assistance in spiritual counseling. In sixteen years of ministry he had become such an integral part of community life that his sudden death hit the lives of not only his congregation, but the entire city.

He was buried on the Thursday following his death. The funeral was conducted in the church by Rabbi Frank Rosenthal. Rabbi Rosenthal was dressed in a Geneva gown and spoke from the epistles of Paul as well as the psalms of David. He spoke with dignity and deep feeling. He, too, grieved. Frank Post had been a good friend and colleague. In many ways the rabbi perhaps had an insight into the mind and soul of this Baptist minister that few, if any, in the Baptist congregation possessed. Deep sorrow has a majesty. The words the rabbi spoke were eloquent, comforting, and spiritual.

two

THE FOLLOWING SUNDAY, the first after the minister's death, the morning service was conducted by Dr. William Lester and the Rev. Theodore H. Horton, both of the First Presbyterian Church. It was a difficult assignment. What do you say at a time like this? How do you listen when you can't really believe that he is gone?

Reality came when the church moderator stood in the pulpit and announced a special meeting of the church membership for the purpose of electing a pulpit committee to be charged with finding a new minister. The announcement was to be repeated for the next two weeks as required by the church constitution. On the Thursday evening following the third announcement, the meeting would be held.

How does a church elect a pulpit committee? It seems rather simple. In reality it becomes very complex. Suddenly a church body that considered itself to be homogeneous discovers it has a variety of special interests.

In the vestibule of the church, in the halls of the educational building, in the women's meetings, remarks are heard that indicate heavy thinking is taking place.

"Something has to be done about the young people's work."

"Let's get back to the Bible."

"Let's have new, fresh, modern thinking."

"I hope we're not going to get involved in the Negro problem."

"Or Vietnam."

There are phone calls, casual, impromptu meetings. Potential candidates are "felt out."

The First Baptist Church in its own refined, dignified way is up to its ears in the good old American game of election eve politics.

There was a large turnout at the meeting. The moderator read the by-laws of the church relating to the election of a pulpit committee. Inasmuch as the by-laws were rather general in nature, stating only that the committee should consist of five members, house rules were adopted to suit the occasion. These took considerable discussion and debate, but finally it was decided that:

Nominations would be taken from the floor.

Each member would vote for five nominees.

The top five vote-getters would constitute the committee. Election would require at least 50 percent of the total vote.

After the ground rules were established, the meeting was thrown open for nominations. Instantly, people jumped up for recognition. Finally, after twenty-nine names had been put forward, the nominations were closed.

Surprisingly, four people received over 50 percent of the vote on the first ballot, and the fifth received it on the second.

The committee had been elected. They were charged with their task. The church body settled back to await the arrival of their new minister.

three

Jack Aird looked around at the four others of the pulpit committee sitting with him in the study of the church. He wondered why he was there. When the first shock of the tragic event had worn off, and the congregation began making plans for a new minister, he had stood back and watched from a distance. His three years as a member in the staid old church made him a relative newcomer, and he observed with almost detached curiosity as the membership creaked into motion on what was considered the most critical problem facing a Baptist church.

After all, congregational autonomy presents a unique problem to Baptists and other similarly governed churches. The replacement of a pastor in a Roman Catholic, Episcopalian, Methodist, or many other churches is made by the responsible, well-qualified hierarchy, who in infinite wisdom, fortified with divine guidance, expediency, and hunch, match the pastor with the church. The choice is accepted without question — at least without undue resistance. But the First Baptist Church of Cedar City had no bishop to make the choice. As a Baptist church, it was a slave to freedom with the right of every member to cast an equal and independent ballot in the choice of a minister.

Aird's curiosity had not been directed toward the composition of the pulpit committee, since he assumed its members would come from the patriarchs of the church, but rather to the procedure by which they would go about this seemingly impossible task of finding someone to satisfy all of the congregation. He soon discovered, however, that his interest in this matter was to become more than casual and that he was to play a part far different from that of a curious bystander. The first intimation came after a Sunday morning service when a hint was dropped that several members of the church were considering him a good prospect for the committee. The thought had seemed so ludicrous that he laughed when it was mentioned. No one, but no one, was more ignorant than he about how to attack such a job. With his lack of firsthand knowledge of the church in Cedar City, he was probably one of the most unlikely persons to put on the committee. Then, a week later, his wife Dorothy mentioned that she had been asked about his willingness to serve on the committee if elected. With the confidence and familiarity born of twenty-five years of marriage, she had immediately assured her questioner that he would. It was no great surprise, then, on the night of the church meeting that he was nominated and elected to the committee. What was more surprising was that the pulpit committee elected him to be its chairman.

Now, at the committee's first meeting, he glanced around at the other four members. He knew them all, of course, but now, perhaps from habit formed from countless civic and business meetings in the past, he appraised them anew. Sitting across from him was Dick Walker. Dick was a corporate auditor for the electric utility company, Consumers Power. He was probably in his early forties and had an easy smile and ready wit. A family man, not too religious, he was more the board of trustee type than the deacon type. Aird was glad that Walker was on the committee. He would have a level head and could compromise if necessary.

Sitting next to Dick was Alice Larcher. Alice had been on the pulpit committee which sixteen years previously had brought Dr. Post to the church. Also, her husband was moderator, which in a Baptist church meant that he coordinated all the lay activities and was the lay leader. Alice was a diminutive, white-haired schoolteacher, who was even now preparing for retirement. She had a young face, twinkling eyes, and quiet charm. She had a mind of her own and a schoolteacher's love of meticulous detail. She would make her own decisions, but she would also provide some badly needed experience.

Marion Frazer was at the far end of the table. She was to be the secretary of the committee. Marion was the only one of the five who didn't have an occupation, unless you considered maintaining a home for a husband and three children, providing taxi service for her non-driving teen-agers, and volunteering for hospital and welfare activities an occupation. Then, of course, there were the clubs — The University Women and The Dames and Matrons. What, he wondered, was the difference between a dame and a matron? He glanced over at her. She was busy preparing her papers for the first meeting. Dorothy and he were in the same social group in the church as Marion and her husband, Gil. He had enjoyed their company whenever they had been together, but working with an individual was different from meeting socially within a group. He thought back to the couple of occasions when he had had an opportunity to talk with her. She had a vibrant manner about her, and when she spoke her voice had a sense of urgency. Self-assured and intelligent, she was not afraid to face and grapple with a situation that affected her family's welfare. He wasn't sure that they would always agree, but she would do a good job.

The fifth member of the committee was sitting next to him. Dar Wood was the youngest of the group and in the life of the church fell into the category known as the "young married couples." He was a tall, well-built, ruggedly handsome type of man. He had the combination of a warm personality and a personal ambitious drive that spoke well for the future of the soft water company that he owned and operated. Dar was also the chairman of the board of deacons and had suddenly been thrust into the responsibility of providing the spiritual leadership of the church. Six months before, when he had been elected chairman of the board of deacons, the idea that the position would entail such responsibility was extremely remote. Surely, if this had been anticipated, someone more mature and experienced would have been chosen. But in a unique and mysterious way, Dar had grown overnight into the job and was meeting the challenge as well as anyone could have done. What his thinking was about the church's requirements for a minister was hard to predict. However, whatever he concluded they were, he would fight hard to see that the standards were met.

Aird looked at his watch and called the meeting to order. "Dr. Worden will be here in a few minutes. I expect that he will be able to outline to us the best approach for kicking this thing off."

"Jack, before Dr. Worden gets here I have something to say that might interest the rest of the committee." Alice spoke in a quiet, moderated voice that had a trace of benignity, but Aird was to find out before many meetings had gone by that she was a five-foot, one-inch Rock of Gibraltar. "You all know, I am sure," she went on, "that Dr. Worden is the Executive Secretary of the Baptist Convention in our state. As such, he is the source through which we will receive most of our information regarding possible candidates, and I suppose all the resumés will be, or should be, channeled through him."

"That sounds reasonable," observed Dar. "I mean, if he's the head man in the state, he ought to be the one to give us the guidance we need."

"Yes, I suppose so," continued Alice, "but you must realize that he can't send us the resumés of every minister in our denomination, or even those of everyone who is interested in making a change. Therefore, he does a certain amount of screening and sends us only those which he feels are most suitable for our church."

"What's significant about that?" It was Dick's question.

Alice pursed her lips. "The significant thing is that while our church has been quite liberal — at least during the ministry of Dr. Post — the great majority of Baptist churches in our state, and probably Dr. Worden too, are conservative in doctrine. It's very likely that his idea of a suitable minister for our church will be completely different from what we have been used to or even want."

There was a silence when she had finished. This issue — theological conservatism vs. theological liberalism — was one the rest of the committee had not known existed within their denomination. In the hectic months ahead, they were to learn that it would be a major obstacle in the efforts of the committee to find a suitable man.

four

Baptists, in a rather mystic way, believe that their search for a minister has divine guidance and that the man finally called will have been directed to the pulpit by the hand of God. The reasonableness of this belief is open to question. But certainly no denomination is more in need of God's help.

The Baptists' love of the democratic process and their guarding of the rights of the individual set the tone for a ministerial selection process that is bumbling, illogical, and dependent on happenstance. The search and selection are made by a committee that more often than not has no experience or training for such a task. Then to compound the problem, their selection is voted on by a general church membership that is equally unqualified to make a decision.

The state executive secretary is the only concession that Baptists make to reality or to efficient administrative practices. His office serves as a clearinghouse for the personnel records of all ministers within the Baptist state convention. Also, through contact with the secretaries in other states he has available to him the records of all other ministers in the denomination. The men appointed as state secretaries are invariably former ministers of substantial reputation and ability. They can often exert considerable influence on the pulpit committee's choice. The degree to which a pulpit committee uses this service, however, depends on how responsive it is to "outside" help, and in many cases the secretary is ignored completely.

Because the Cedar City Baptist church committee was in no mood to turn down any help from anyone, they sat across from Dr. Worden in that first meeting and appraised him intently as he reviewed for them just what was involved in this new task.

Worden had the look of a successful man. He was the prototype of a bank president. Well groomed, he carried his clothes gracefully on his six-foot frame. If the middle-age paunch was present, it was at least balanced by an overall bearing of muscular strength and physical well-being. In addition, Robert Worden had the carefully modulated voice of a suburban minister and the easy smile and casual composure that discouraged antagonism and bred compromise.

As he related the pitfalls of all pulpit committees, his voice revealed no sign of solicitation or condescension, even though what he had to say must have been said many times before to many other groups.

"There will be lots of people giving you free advice. It won't be worth much." He looked around the room. A smile teased at his lips. "You'd be surprised how many people know just the right candidate for the job. Also, some ministers might contact you directly indicating that they feel 'a special and peculiar call to your church.' " The smile finally broke through. "Don't jump at any of these offers. Take your time. Determine what you really want. I have got, or can obtain, complete dossiers on any man in the denomination. Study carefully the available dossier on every candidate that you consider."

"Have you brought any of this information with you?"

"Well, I've got a few here." He reached into his briefcase and brought out a sheaf of papers. "This will give you an idea of what information is available."

Worden passed a resumé to each of the committee members and they studied the papers with interest. Included in each resumé were the vital statistics usually found in personal biographical sketches as well as a record of work history. In addition, however, the resumés included a number of carefully phrased theological questions which required answers by the applicant. Then on the final page was a summary of six appraisals submitted by associates or others well acquainted with the man being appraised.

"Here's one," said Worden, "who has a lot to offer a church such as yours. He's relatively young — forty-one — good-looking. Lots of hair. He has a good platform manner and preaches a good sermon. He's a real personable guy. People like him and he gets things done. I don't know if you can get him, but he would be worth going after."

"Where did he go to school?" This was Alice Larcher's first question and was to be the one that she invariably used first in appraising candidates throughout the length of the search.

"Wheaton College. Of course, I could be a little biased on this fellow. That's my school too, you know."

Worden laughed in a manner that indicated that he would be understood, but Aird couldn't help thinking of Alice's concern relative to conservatism. Wheaton was decidedly a conservative school.

He addressed himself to Dr. Worden. "You know, our church has open membership. Would this man find this acceptable?"

"I don't think his present church has open membership, but I don't think it would be a major stumbling block to him. You know you're not as alone on this issue as you might think. More and more churches are doing away with the requirement of baptism by immersion for membership."

"Dr. Worden," Marion spoke in that slow, earnest manner that was to become her trademark in the months to come, "we have this sort of a coffeehouse thing called the 'Back Door.' It's open every Saturday night in the basement of our church. Each week there is a teen-age rock and roll band and the kids from all over the city come to dance." She looked at him closely. "What would your minister think about this?"

Worden sat quietly for a moment, a little frown of concentration on his face. "Well, dancing in the church might create a problem. Yes, he might not be able to buy that." Then he brightened. "Of course, if the dance is used to get the kids to come to Sunday school and church, he may see the value of it."

"There are no strings attached," Dick Walker almost growled the comment. "All we ask is to give the kids a chance to get off the street and have a good time."

Worden looked at him thoughtfully and then stared down at the resumé in front of him as though trying to reach for something in the biographical data.

"Of course, one really never knows," he murmured softly. "Things have changed so quickly in the past few years. Values change. One is hard pressed to know what one believes in at any given time." In that instance, Dr. Worden was giving the committee an insight into a struggle that was taking place in the consciences of many Baptist ministers throughout the denomination.

Later, after Dr. Worden had excused himself, the committee drew up guidelines for the "ideal candidate." The man they wanted would be between ages thirty-five and forty-five. His main forte would be preaching, followed in order by pastoral guidance, youth work, administration, and community relations. Unwritten guidelines, which later discussion indicated were already in the minds of various members of the committee, were that the candidate must be a graduate of a fully accredited college, have a good personal appearance, be dynamic in nature, be married, and not have attended an ultraconservative college or seminary.

The committee adjourned, satisfied that their search had gotten off to a good start. Now that they knew what they were looking for, the job was just a matter of finding the right man.

This proved to be much more difficult than any of them imagined.

five

The next several meetings of the committee following their session with Dr. Worden were spent in studying the resumés that he had furnished to them. All in all, before the search was completed, the committee read over one hundred resumés. At first these were carefully studied and read individually by each of the five prior to meeting together, and then the resumés were read aloud once again in the weekly meetings so that comments could be made and a joint evaluation made. This was a painfully slow task. Some of the resumés were handwritten and barely legible. Others were messy with erasures and smudges. Many provided answers and comments that were muddled or ambiguous. During the reading of one such resumé Dick Walker lost his cool. "You know, I can't figure out these people," he said. "It seems to me, if they are really looking for a change, or even remotely interested in one, that they would take the time to prepare a resumé that is at least reasonably clear. After all, at this point, the only introduction we have to these people is through their resumés and a lot of names are being thrown out just

PRAY A PRAYER OF DEDICATION

"O God, put a new and right spirit within me . . . Open my lips, and my mouth shall show forth thy praise." —Psalm 51:10, 15

When you have confessed your sins, and received His forgiveness, you should then dedicate yourself anew to God. As a result, you will then become a stronger witness for Him.

Guide me, Heavenly Father, as I endeavor to witness for thee and to serve thee, after the example of thy Son, in His name. Amen.

No. PF-10 Church World Press, Inc.
Cleveland, Ohio 44113

THE POWER OF PRAYER

Prayer is the greatest source of power available to man. But, are you making the most of it? Take a few minutes each day to develop your prayer life, using these five types of prayer as examples.

PRAY A PRAYER OF THANKSGIVING

"To thee, O God . . . I give thanks and praise." —Daniel 2:23

How often do you express your thanks to God for all of His benefits to you? As you express your gratitude for those things He has done, He will hear, and will bless you.

Almighty God, I am grateful for all of the bountiful gifts that have come from thee; hear my words of praise, in Christ's name. Amen.

PRAY A PRAYER OF CONFESSION

"Have mercy on me, O God . . . and cleanse me from my sin." —Psalm 51:1, 2

If you would seek spiritual cleansing from within, then you need to ask the forgiveness of God. As you confess your sins in the spirit of penitence, you will experience His forgiving power.

Dear God, grant me thy forgiveness for the sins I have committed. Be merciful and cleanse me from within, in the Saviour's name. Amen.

PRAY A PRAYER OF PETITION

"Hear my prayer, O Lord; give ear to my supplications." —Psalm 143:1

Pray to God for spiritual help with which to face the problems of life. He will grant you those things, including inner strength and guidance, which you need each day.

Sustain me, O Father, with thy spiritual power and grant me that inner peace and direction which only You can give, through Jesus Christ my Lord. Amen.

PRAY A PRAYER OF INTERCESSION

"I do not pray for these only, but also for those who believe in me." —John 17:20

When you pray for someone else, God sends His power into that person's soul and seeks to help him. Pray that those who are ill, and those facing diverse problems, may feel his spiritual presence watching over them.

Eternal God, send thy power and thy peace unto those who are in need of thy help. Be especially near to those about whom I am concerned, in the name of Christ. Amen.

because they don't take the time to prepare something that we can read."

"Or understand," added Alice Larcher. "How would you gauge the suitability of this man? 'Conservative in doctrine but liberal in spirit.' "

"Well, now," said Marion, "I think he means . . ." She struggled to put her thoughts into words and then lamely said, "I guess I don't know what he means." It was too bad that she failed in the attempt because the same comment appeared in one form or another in a great many self-descriptions. Perhaps the most unusual was the prospective candidate who bravely described himself as "a conservative liberal well-grounded."

Screening candidates by the references provided in the dossiers proved to be no easier. As a rule, the resumés included six reference ratings as to the candidate's qualifications in those attributes deemed to be most pertinent to the ministerial calling. These evaluations were summarized and graded in the resumé and rated: Unsatisfactory, Satisfactory, or Very Good. It appeared at first that the Cedar City committee was particularly blessed in receiving only those resumés of above average or outstanding candidates. Very seldom did a reference indicate otherwise. Later on, when the committee had the opportunity to meet and interview personally some of the candidates whose resumés they had received, it became obvious that the yardstick of measurement used by those furnishing the references was, in most cases, much shorter than that used by the committee. In fact, on several occasions the candidate met personally by the committee was so dissimilar from his resumé that the committee made it a point to review once again the dossier to assure themselves they had not initially misread the document. This resulted in an interesting observation. The obvious weaknesses revealed in a prospective candidate by visiting him in his own church and by personal interview were often buried in guarded phrases beneath the platitudes and praises in the dossier. As the committee became more adept at resumé reading, they were able to dig out and examine such innocent looking comments as "Mr. X is quiet, earnest, and purposeful." (Mr. X turned out to be introverted, self-conscious, and decidedly lacking in personality.)

"Mr. Y's messages are not emotional but he preaches the solid meat discourses." (Mr. Y's sermon almost put the committee to sleep.)

"Sometimes his drive to achieve the goals has offended people. He would do well in a position where contacts were not of too long duration." (These two revealing sentences were extracted from a long paragraph which was overwhelmingly enthusiastic about the candidate's abilities in achieving results.)

When one cannot decipher the professional jargon of the writer of the resumé and is not completely confident in the supplementary references provided, one must find some other means of evaluation. The committee took refuge in statistics, searching out those statistics appealing to their own personal bias. Candidates were screened on the basis of age, appearance, marital status, and schools attended. A man of forty-five was too old. A man under thirty-five was too young. No single man was to be considered. A strong education from an accredited college or university was a must. Graduates of southern fundamentalistic Bible colleges were out.

Perhaps this type of screening was unfair, but it did serve its purpose. It screened so well that by the time the first batch of prospects had been sifted, there were very few names left.

Fortunately, time and experience brought to the committee a degree of sophistication in resumé reading. The committee found that the great majority of Baptist clergymen typed themselves by the manner in which they prepared their dossiers. While personal interviews sometimes showed candidates to be less than their dossier indicated, very few candidates, when interviewed, proved to be superior to their resumés.

In spite of this, the use of resumés was the most valuable tool the committee had. There was the obvious saving of time and money that would have been spent for personal interviews. Also, the committee was able to make evaluations free of pressure since the subjects of their resumés did not usually know that they were being considered. There was no obligation on the part of the committee to explain to a candidate the reason for rejection; although from a practical point of view, an explanation to the source providing the resumé as to the reason the candidate was unsuitable stopped the flow of similar-type resumés and enabled the committee's sources to be more selective in what they furnished. The committee learned that once a minister knew he was being considered the matter was no longer objective. While the great majority of ministers were very discreet in showing even the slightest sign of undue interest, one or two were not averse to using some psychological tricks in this divine game of ministerial calling.

The first batch of resumés read by the Cedar City

committee showed four promising candidates – one each in Indiana, Iowa, Massachusetts, and Michigan. The one from Massachusetts looked particularly good, met all the ground rules that the committee had established, and appeared to be ideally suited for the Cedar City church. To find such a candidate so early in the search was more than any of the group had hoped for, and a letter was sent off immediately by Marion to Massachusetts. There was no further activity, no further review of applicants, while the committee waited for an answer to its first contact. Unfortunately, when the answer did come, it proved to be the first in a long series of disappointments. The candidate's reply stated that he had just been called to a new church and "cannot consider a move at the present time." The committee now turned its attention to the man from Michigan.

six

Hiring a Baptist minister is a cloak-and-dagger experience. The last thing a minister wants is for his congregation to find out prematurely that he is considering a "call" to another church. Heaven help the poor soul who has to face a congregation that knows he was jilted by a pulpit committee. For this reason all contacts made by the pulpit committee to prospective candidates are done in the most discreet way. Phone calls are made only to his home and never to the candidate's office. All correspondence is sent to the home and marked personal and confidential.

The initial correspondence, while specific and pragmatic in describing the needs of the inquiring church and the benefits the church is prepared to offer, is deliberately obtuse in regards to specifics about the minister. "We are writing to determine your possible interest . . . It is understood that your favorable response to our letter in no way indicates a commitment either on your part or on ours." The replies are usually equally vague — that is, unless there is no interest whatsoever, and then most ministers are kind enough to give a flat "no." More often the reply is "yes" and almost always qualified in some way. There is the cautious yes, "I love my ministry here and the people are wonderful, but. . . ." There is the reluctant yes that ingeniously puts all the blame for the move on God: "I am happy in my ministry here, but if it is God's will for me to move. . . ." Then there is the devil-may-care yes: "My conscience is clear. I have accomplished my mission here and am ready for a new challenge." There is also the cool, hard-to-get, subtly concealed yes: "I am really not interested in a move at the present time. We are having a very successful ministry here; however, in the interest of my family and looking forward to their college years, I would probably consider a move if the conditions were properly challenging."

Whatever the answer, the one certainty is that the minister who encourages further contact with the pulpit committee is walking on eggs until a firm decision is made.

For this reason, the Cedar City committee established several ground rules regarding the visiting of a prospect in his home church. The first was that no minister would be visited unless he had first indicated his interest to the pulpit committee. The second was that a prospect's church would not be visited without first clearing the date with the minister. The first makes sense if for no other reason than to save time and money for the pulpit committee (and this gets to be of major importance in a drawn-out search). The second is a courtesy that would seem to be a normal act of graciousness and fair play. Yet, many ministers indicated that "sneak visits" by pulpit committees were quite commonplace. One minister advised that sneak visits do not work and assured the committee, "I can spot a pulpit committee as soon as they walk into the sanctuary." Another said firmly that he would not recognize or allow an interview with a delegation who came to his church without an invitation. With these two ground rules the committee was free from embarrassment on this score, but plenty of other things happened.

Dick and Dar made the first trip, which was to visit the Michigan candidate. Both of them were used to meeting people in their business life. Dick, as an auditor, had made a profession of knowing the right question to ask. Dar, in his business, dealt with the public daily. In spite of their backgrounds, they were both obviously apprehensive about the assignment — and the others on the committee, if forced to answer, would have admitted a feeling of relief that the first visit was being made by someone else.

Both were full of questions. "What do we do when we enter the church? Do we sign the guest register?"

"No!"

"Well, we'll be strange faces. You know what these Baptist churches are like. They'll try and make members out of us."

"Tell them you're from out of town and just passing through."

"And how do we get to talk with the minister?"

"He'll be at the door shaking hands as you leave. That shouldn't be any problem at all."

"Yeah, but everyone else will be there too. And if he wants to keep this hush-hush, that will be no time to announce that we are the visiting pulpit committee."

"You'll think of something."

"Then if we do get to talk to him, what do we say? I mean, what do we know about theology? If we could possibly think of a question, we wouldn't even know if he gave the right answer."

This went on for quite some time. Alice tried to think back sixteen years to the time she was on the pulpit committee before. "We didn't seem to have these problems then. But we really didn't do much looking. We sort of settled on Dr. Post and that was that."

It was finally agreed that the only instructions for Dick and Dar were to play it cool. Maybe the first visit would be a failure. If so, it would be charged to experience and the committee would be better prepared for the next.

The Tuesday following the visit, the pulpit committee met. Dick and Dar weren't the same two nervously unsure men of the meeting a week ago. To paraphrase an old gospel hymn, "a wonderful change in their lives had been wrought."

Dick gave the report. It was apparent as soon as he started to talk that he had something to say and was enjoying saying it. It was also apparent that he was going to stretch the enjoyment out to a considerable length. He started at the beginning and brought the committee along the highway from Cedar City to his destination. "You know, we wondered why Reverend Leeds would be interested in our church. I mean, he's already getting as much salary as we can offer, and his present church is as large in numbers as ours. But when we saw that town, there was no doubt in our minds why he wanted to leave. Boy! What a place!" Then he went on to describe the factories and smudge that made up the town.

"What happened when you went in?" Marion asked. "Did you sign the guest register? Did you have to wear a visitor's ribbon? Did anyone say anything to you?"

"Well, that's a funny thing. We didn't have to do anything. Nobody said a word to us. You know, come to think of it, it wasn't a very friendly place. But I'll get to that later. Let me tell you how the church building looked as we drove up to it."

Dick went back to pick up the broken thread in his dialogue. "The usher took us down the main isle and sat us in about the middle of the sanctuary, and you know that minister spotted us as soon as we walked in."

"Oh, now, you probably imagined that."

"Nope, he spotted us as soon as we walked in. You gotta remember he knew we were coming and was probably looking for us. And how many times do two strange men without any womenfolk walk into our sanctuary?" He had a point, and the group relinquished any further attempt at argument and reconciled themselves to a long description of the church service.

"Pretty standard type of service. Much like our own. His sermon, which he gave with extensive use of notes, wasn't bad. Nothing to write home about, but nothing to get disturbed about either. But, you know, we were a little surprised about him. I mean, he looked somewhat different than his picture, wouldn't you say, Dar?"

Dar roused himself over on the other side of the room. "Yeah, he was a little balder than that picture we got with the resumé."

"And smaller," added Dick. "He was smaller than we expected." The committee was to find out as time went on that almost all of the ministers visited were balder than their pictures and shorter or fatter.

"Well," said Alice, "I don't think it's too important how much hair he's got."

"I don't know," Marion spoke a little hesitantly, as though not too sure how strong her point was. "I'd like our minister to have hair."

"It wasn't until the service ended that things got a little sticky," Dick was back on his report. "As the congregation started to leave the church, we sort of hung back so as to bring up the rear. Do you realize just how slow some people move in getting away from church? Well, we hung back as long as we could, but we still couldn't outwait some of those people, and after a while we found ourselves up to the door shaking hands with the minister."

Dar unwound across the room and said, "That's right, but that man knew right away who we were even before we said our names. And it didn't phase him one bit."

"He sure did," Dick picked up the story again. "He just shook our hands, said he was glad to see us, and asked us to wait for him in his study."

"And how did your interview go? Did you manage to find the right things to ask?"

Dick laughed — almost sheepishly. "That's a funny thing. It wasn't until we were on our way home that we realized that we hadn't really asked any questions at all. Oh, he asked some questions of us about Cedar City and our church, which we answered. But regarding him and his church, he'd sort of pose a question and then he'd give the answer. And you know, he covered everything we wanted to know and then some." Dick looked over at Dar. "How about you giving the group a rundown on how he seemed to stack up?"

"Well," Dar crossed his legs and draped one arm over the back of the overstuffed chair he was sitting in. "It seemed to us from what he said during the interview, and also from his sermon, that he was quite a down-to-earth guy. He didn't wear a robe, although he said he would wear one if that's what the church wanted. He didn't have much to say, pro or con, about community stuff—civil rights and all that. In fact, he wasn't really fired up about anything. Seemed like a real nice guy and we thought that he'd get along with people. He seemed pretty doggone interested in coming to our church."

"What is your recommendation about this man?" asked Aird. "Should we follow up on this thing? Would you say he's a hot prospect?"

"Well, like Dar said, he's a real nice guy and he sure wouldn't get our church in any trouble."

"But what do you recommend?"

Dick looked over at Dar. "Dar and I have started a routine that we intend to use on everyone we interview. After we get away from the interview, we don't say anything about our impressions until we have had an opportunity to sit down and write individual reports, including recommendations."

"And what did you decide on this man?" Aird pressed.

"It's funny, but both Dar and I came up with the same answer. We decided that Leeds should be put on the back burner. We wouldn't say an outright rejection. Maybe he's the best we will find. But at this stage of the game, we'd like to aim for someone a little more of a dynamo than he seemed to be."

seven

THE NORTHERN ROUTE from Cedar City to California runs reasonably close to Omaha, Nebraska, where Rev. S. W. Bauldry resided. The fact that Omaha was a considerable distance from Cedar City had at first created somewhat of a problem in planning a committee visit. Air travel was expensive, and the distance was too great to drive on a weekend. Now, however, a planned October vacation trip by Aird and his wife, Dorothy, to the west coast presented an opportunity for a stopoff in Omaha, provided that the timing could be suitably arranged. An exchange of letters with Mr. Bauldry took care of that.

The Airds arrived in Omaha on a Saturday evening and arose early Sunday morning in order to make the 9:30 service. It was a bright, crisp, clear autumn day. They took their time driving through town, checking the road map, and picking up landmarks that would lead to their destination. Even so, they arrived twenty minutes before the scheduled start of the service, and rather than go in early, they continued to drive around the neighborhood to kill time. In doing so, they got lost. When they finally got back to the church, they were ushered to their seats barely in time for the invocation. Aird looked around cautiously. He wondered if he and Dorothy were the only strange faces there. Probably not. The auditorium was about two-thirds full and certainly on any Sunday morning there must be a number of visitors. He looked curiously at the chancel. It was so arranged that the choir sat in a slightly raised section directly below a large replica of the cross. Several super-sized straight-backed chairs winged out on the front part of the platform. The one on the left held the minister, or that is, would have held him if he hadn't been at that moment standing, singing the opening hymn with the congregation. And he was singing! As the pulpit committee's visits became more frequent, Aird found that some ministers – certainly not a majority, but an annoying number – stood and stared at the congregation during the singing of the hymns or just plain got lost. But Pastor Bauldry was singing. His lips were moving. No distinctive sound could be heard from his direction, nor did his face show any animation, but of a certainty he was singing.

At the close of the hymn, he stepped forward to the pulpit, which was located front and center. Now his face took on expression. Aird mentally compared it with the picture that had accompanied Bauldry's resumé. Yes, his hair was a little thinner, and yet he somehow looked younger than his picture. His face was rather gaunt, and his mouth, which was not particularly strong, was set in a rather winsome smile, which seemed to project on the words he spoke.

After prayers, responsive reading, and the singing of

the choir, he stepped forward again to give the weekly announcements. It's hard to look folksy in a black robe, but it seemed to Aird that Bauldry, standing there, announcing the potluck dinner for Wednesday evening, seemed downright homespun. When he spoke about Brother Watkins being laid up in the hospital and asked for the prayers of the congregation, he sounded like he really cared. There was warmth in his voice as he spoke of events in the lives of the church families during the past week. Of sorrows experienced: "We share in the bereavement of the __________ family in the sudden passing away of Jim." Of success attained: "It was a thrill to pick up the evening paper last Thursday and see the announcement of the appointment of Bob __________ to the position of __________." His voice was animated and clearly expressed his feelings of happiness, sadness, or enthusiasm as he recounted events in the life of the church.

A few minutes later, when Bauldry gave his sermon, it seemed to Aird that he was hearing and seeing an entirely different man. His almost musical voice, which had changed in cadence and pitch depending on the mood, now was well-controlled, perfectly timed, and came out in a steady, monotonous drone. Every once in a while, at what seemed like a predetermined spot, his right arm would shoot out, as though he were flinging his hand at someone in the balcony. He started preaching at twenty-five minutes after the hour. Aird did some mental calculations. As the service was scheduled to end on the hour, with five minutes allowed for the closing hymn and prayer, Bauldry would speak exactly thirty minutes. As it turned out, he spoke thirty-two minutes.

At the close of the service, the Airds flowed with the current and soon found themselves at the front door of the church shaking hands with the man they had traveled so many miles to meet. His voice was now almost singsong, "Well, well, the Airds. We have been expecting you. My office is over in the educational wing. Why don't you sort of drift over in that direction, and when I can get away from the door, my wife and I will join you." The educational building was a recent addition which formed a wing to the original building. The Cedar City church had gone through a similar building program not too long ago, and the Airds spent their time comparing the two buildings while trying to remain as inconspicuous as possible.

Remnants of the Sunday school were still departing. Aird grabbed his wife's arm and guided her into what appeared to be an empty classroom, only to collide with a woman leaving by the same door. Introductions followed. She was a Sunday school teacher. Also, she was inquisitive. A barrage of questions followed.

The Airds answered reluctantly. No, they would not be in town long. They were just pasing through. Yes, they were Baptists. "Whereabouts?" Aird looked at his wife in discomfort. She was no help at all. He lamely answered the question, only to face another.

"Oh, is that near Johnstown?" The Sunday school teacher had a good friend in Johnstown. With this common bond, the distance separating her from the Airds now diminished from hundreds of miles to the forty miles that Johnstown was from Cedar City. She insisted on showing them the rest of the educational building. It would be no trouble at all. Aird looked again at his wife. She apparently wasn't sharing his embarrassment and, in fact, appeared to have found a new friend. He decided to shed his concern, too. After all, there was little more the woman could know about them than she had already found out. He relaxed and listened as she took them on a tour of the classrooms, accompanied by a running dialogue of the entire church program. They went through the primary, intermediate, and senior sections of the building and were admiring, with their guide, the small chapel just erected when Bauldry and his wife walked up. Aird's embarrassment returned but was tempered by curiosity as he wondered how Bauldry would ease out of what appeared to be a "caught in the cookie jar" event. It did not phase Bauldry a bit.

"Yes, we have met Mr. and Mrs. Aird." A soft smile passed across his face. "They have been waiting to see me."

"Oh," her face dropped. Then she smiled again and turned to the Airds. "Well, I was glad to be able to show you around. I hope you can come back and visit our church again."

"Thank you. Thank you very much. You have been very kind."

She said good-bye and left. Bauldry led the way to his office, ushered the Airds in, and left them there with his wife while he removed his robe.

The office was spacious as such things go. Carpeting covered the floor, and a sofa and several easy chairs provided a sitting-room area away from business sections of the room. Aird and Dorothy sat on the sofa, and Mrs. Bauldry sat in one of the easy chairs below a landscape of early western America. Bauldry, when he joined them, pulled over one of the easy chairs so that he was sitting directly across from Aird. Now, seen in a business suit, without the concealing folds of his robe, he seemed much slighter of build. Also, strangely enough, considering his slim, trim figure, he looked shorter than he actually was. He inquired as to their trip. Then he mentioned a close friend and colleague of his who had only a year ago left Nebraska to take a church in the eastern part of their state. Finally, the discussion got around to Cedar City's pulpit committee's search for a minister. Questions were asked about Cedar City — about the church, the manner in which the services were handled, how the church was managing without a minister. Finally he asked, "Do you have open membership?"

It was asked intently in a controlled tone of voice that only emphasized the importance he placed on the question.

"Why, yes, we do." It seemed a rather surprising question at the time although Aird discovered later, as the search went on, that many Baptist ministers were still struggling with this question. In fact, with some it was not a question at all — only baptized converts could join the church, and then only if baptism was by immersion.

At Aird's answer a worried frown creased his face. "I suppose I could live with that, but I must admit that I find it awkward."

The last word came out almost as a sigh. Aird looked at him silently and was grateful to hear Dorothy speak. "We certainly don't discourage converts and new members from going through the ritual of baptism, but it does seem a little harsh to refuse membership to a person purely on the basis of his refusal to take part in a ceremony that is obviously only symbolic, even though he professes acceptance of Christ and the church."

"Yes, well, a colleague whom I respect very much has recently sent me a copy of a paper that he will soon have published that argues very well the case for open membership." He smiled almost apologetically. "I guess I could live with open membership if my people really felt that was what they wanted."

He spoke so humbly and seemed so painfully honest in his search for the right answer to this question that Aird felt he needed to explain that their own congregation was not completely of one mind on theological questions. "I guess you could say that we are made up of liberals, conservatives, and a lot that don't know which they are. What we really need is a minister that can meet the needs of all of us."

"Be all things to all men, I guess." This was the first comment that Mrs. Bauldry had made since the start of the discussion. Aird knew she was quoting from one of Paul's epistles, but he couldn't remember if Paul was for it or against it. It was obvious though, from the tone of her voice, that Mrs. Bauldry certainly felt that the straight and narrow path could hardly be stretched or bent to accept much deviation.

Aird changed the subject and asked the attitude of the Omaha church regarding black integration.

"You may have noticed," said Bauldry, "the large Negro section just east of our church. The colored have been creeping in this direction for quite a while, and the day will soon come when they will be living in this neighborhood. We've thought about it a lot, and I suppose if a Negro family wanted to join our church that they would be accepted."

"Do you have any Negro members now?"

"No, we do not."

The question regarding the acceptance of Negroes became standard in the interviews wherever Aird went, and the answer was almost invariably the same. In only one church did he find that Negroes were already members. This particular church had one Negro member. She sang in the choir and happened to be attending a local state university working on her Ph.D.

The subject changed and reached a level more easily and comfortably discussed — how to keep the young people after they reach college age, what to do to freshen up Sunday school programs. Bauldry answered each question carefully in language that suggested that he was pulling out phrases from a mental file and would carefully refile the data in its proper place to be used again when the occasion so required. Eventually, the discussion just seemed to die out. Then, after a pause, Mrs. Bauldry said, "We would love to have you stay for dinner." It wasn't just a courtesy remark. Her voice and expression convinced Aird that she meant it, but the itinerary for him and his wife called for them to be in Grand Forks by nightfall.

Later, driving along the highway, he dictated a report of the visit to Dorothy, who sent it back in longhand to the committee in Cedar City. The conclusion didn't require much thought. Bauldry would be a great guy to know, but as a minister for the First Baptist Church? Well, he would have a nervous breakdown or ulcers before he had been there long enough to get appointed to the Rotary Club Entertainment Committee.

It was three down and one to go.

eight

JUST PRIOR TO THE AIRDS' visiting Bauldry, the committee had received an affirmative response from the Indiana candidate, Rev. David F. Willard. He definitely was interested in hearing more about the Cedar City church. Not only that, he enclosed with his letter several of his published sermons, a church bulletin, and a newsletter. It was the most complete job of documentation that the committee was to receive. The group studied his resumé and accompanying picture carefully. Here might be a winner. He was a tall man — six-foot-two, well-built, with strong, even features. He was thirty-five years old — a little young, but his picture showed that he at least looked mature. He was a graduate of Kalamazoo College, a good school. The data on his wife was skimpy, but what there was sketched the image of the ideal minister's wife — college educated, musically trained, and a mother! No doubt Willard was a prime candidate. It was decided that Alice Larcher and her husband, Hal, would visit Indiana at the earliest possible time.

By the time of the first committee meeting after the

return of the Airds from the west coast, Alice had made her trip and was ready to report.

The pulpit committee meetings had already established a form. The meeting opened with prayer. This was almost always given by Dar Wood – for no particular reason except perhaps that he was chairman of the board of deacons. After the prayer, Marion would open up her folder and extract all the mail sent or received since the last meeting. However, before reading or discussing the mail, Aird asked for the reports of any of the group who had visited a candidate since the last meeting. So it was that they listened now to Alice.

"First of all, we picked a rather unfortunate time to visit Mr. Willard. It was some kind of a homecoming week in his church, and the sermon was delivered by the former pastor, who had been in the church for twenty-two years just prior to Mr. Willard moving in. But then, perhaps it is just as well we visited there this particular week. It gave us a chance to make a pretty good assessment of the true situation down there."

As Alice spoke she leaned forward, straight-backed on the edge of her chair. Her words, as always, were weighed and to the point. As she looked around the room, her eyes were bright and smiling. But even at that, her mouth was strong and firm – almost prim. There was a no-nonsense aura about her that strangely did not contradict the warmth of her eyes or the gentleness of her voice.

"Mr. Willard," Alice continued, "is in a very difficult situation. His predecessor, who had been in the church for twenty-two years, had left the church only to move downtown to a church council position. Having a former minister that close would be unfortunate under even the best of circumstances. The ghost of a minister who has been around twenty-two years can cause enough problems for a new minister even if his predecessor has moved many miles away. But in this particular case the old minister apparently just hasn't been able to give up. He visits his old parish weekly to give advice to his young replacement and, incidentally, to hear the complaints of all the old "pillars" who just don't like the changes that have been made."

"Did he tell you all this?"

"Well, not in so many words. You must remember we were in his service when the old minister was back in the pulpit. Mr. Willard really did nothing but give the announcements and welcome the former minister back home. It was easy to see his discomfort. On the other hand, it was obvious that the so-called guest speaker was really just back home and was in the saddle once again – if only for a day."

"Willard was quite bitter about this?"

"No, not really. He is just too realistic and intelligent for that. As a matter of fact, he didn't mention it at all. After the church service he met us at the door. Really, he was apologizing for our coming on a day that he was not in the pulpit."

"You would think he would have thought about that when he corresponded with you and set up the date for your visit."

"Yes. Well, at any rate, he invited us to stay for the reception that followed the service. We did and had plenty of time to talk to him then. All the social activity in the reception hall was centered on his predecessor and his wife."

"Did you get a chance to talk with Mrs. Willard?"

"I did meet her and their two little girls, but I really didn't get a chance to talk with her. It wasn't till Hal and I were on our way home that I realized that we really hadn't learned very much."

Everyone settled back in his chair. There was a visible sense of disappointment around the room.

In the silence that ensued following her last discouraging remark, Alice opened a manila folder that was on her lap and brought out a sheaf of papers. She handed the top paper to Marion. "This is Mr. Willard's resumé. I'll return it to your file so that it doesn't get lost." She glanced down at the remaining papers in her lap and then looked up and smiled as though relishing the suspense her actions were causing.

"On the ride home that day I kept thinking of the peculiar circumstances surrounding that poor man and the obviously unfriendly church that he was trying to serve. Do you know, no one spoke to us all the time we were there except the minister himself. During the sermon Hal had a coughing spell and had to leave the sanctuary. Of course, Hal can't sit all the way through a sermon under the best of conditions – but nevertheless, he did have this coughing spell and wanted a drink of water. Why, he had a terrible time just trying to find a drinking fountain! The ushers seemed to be completely disinterested, and he finally found a fountain himself in the educational building." Alice shifted her weight and sat back a little in her chair.

"I guess I've allowed myself to drift a little," she said with a short little laugh. "The point that I'm trying to make is that I finally decided that Mr. Willard deserved an opportunity to explain how he happened to be part of such an obviously awkward situation and just what he intended doing about it. So I wrote to him and asked him just that. Marion, here is a copy of the letter I wrote him." She handed over a blue-colored envelope and its contents. "And now I'll read you his answer." She unfolded the remaining paper still in her hand and began to read. It was well-written and a model of restraint, but in essence it confirmed what Alice had already stated about Willard's problems with the former pastor. When she had finished reading, Dar spoke up first.

"Well, now what?"

"It's obvious to me," went on Alice, "that this man just has to get out of the situation that he is in. If he doesn't come to our church, he will have to go somewhere else."

"But is he the type of man that we want? Can he do the job here? After all, Dr. Post was here sixteen years, and undoubtedly the man who comes in will have to face the problem of comparison in just about everything he tries to do."

"Oh, I'm sure he will, but I don't think that's the same at all. In any case, there are some questionable aspects about this man in my mind, too. For example, I don't think that he should have indicated the Sunday in which he was to have a guest speaker in the pulpit as a suitable date for my visit."

"I agree," said Marion. "That sounds like poor planning to me."

"But did he take you into his office and talk with you?" asked Dick. "I found in our visit to our friend in Michigan that the personal interview was of more value in measuring the man than his sermon."

"Well, no, he didn't. But, as I explained, the circumstances certainly weren't the most appropriate for such a discussion. No, I'm not prepared to say he's the man for us, but neither am I prepared to say that he is not. I guess I'm just a little sympathetic to the underdog, and he certainly is the underdog where he is now. My recommendation is that some other members of the committee pay Mr. Willard a visit before we drop him."

So arrangements were made for the Frazers and Airds to visit Willard and his church the following Sunday.

"What did you think of him?" Gil Frazer was asking. The four were walking around the perimeter of the church building killing time while waiting for Willard to finish saying good-bye to the departing congregation at the front door of the sanctuary.

Aird thought Willard had preached an excellent sermon and said so.

"If only he had smiled a little more," sighed Marion. "He had a nice, genuine smile, but he hardly ever used it. He looked so solemn most of the time."

"And what did you think of him?" asked Aird. The question was thrown at Dorothy and Gil, but they weren't to be drawn in.

As Dorothy answered quickly her face radiated impishness. "Oh, no, you don't. You two are the pulpit committee. We are just along for the ride."

By this time they had walked almost completely around the building and were coming up the far side of the educational building when they saw a side entrance and decided to go inside and look around. That's where Willard found them.

"My office is rather small, and I think four of you would find it a little cramped," he said after Aird asked where they might talk. "Perhaps it would be better if we went back to the sanctuary and talked there."

Aird and his wife exchanged glances. Willard had seemed reluctant to have an interview in the first place, but they had reasoned that this was because of his fear of further antagonizing his people. Surely his office, even if small, would be more suitable than sitting in the sanctuary!

Willard directed them to the first two pews. He and Aird sat in the first pew and sort of draped themselves over the back so that they were not seated entirely with their backs to Gil, Marion, and Dorothy, who were sitting in the second pew. Willard seemed to mold his big frame into the contour of the pew with very little trouble, even though he was sitting half-twisted around to face the others. For Aird, however, it seemed wretchedly awkward, and he had hardly sat down when he got back up and relocated a piano stool to sit on.

"Well, what would you like to know?" Willard spoke neither abruptly or curtly. On the other hand, neither could the tone of his voice be called warm or friendly. His voice, his expression, his manner exuded an attitude of something Aird just couldn't define. It wasn't until later — much later — after Dar and Dick had also visited and talked with him, that it finally came through. Dick was the one who expressed it best. "That guy," he said, "is bored."

But at the time of this interview with him, it didn't quite come through that way. Perhaps it just didn't seem possible that a man could be so disinterested about something that so closely related to his future.

Marion voiced appreciation of his superb sermon and his expression seemed to brighten. "I put some work into my sermons—a lot of work. In fact, I've managed to have quite a few of them published," he said.

"Yes," Marion said, "we read those that you were kind enough to include with your letter. They were extremely interesting."

"It takes time. I spend roughly four hours a day on reading and research. Some laymen think good sermons spring from the heart. Actually, they are more often the result of sweat and blood."

"Your sermons seem so decisive on a subject that in many ways is rather indecisive," Aird remarked.

He half-turned in the pew to face Aird. "What is your point?"

"Well, for example, we keep hearing about a never-changing God, and yet the Bible seems to present an ever-changing God—creative, whimsical, jealous, vengeful, murderous, bigoted, understanding, compassionate, forgiving, loving, and then, once again vengeful and as pompous as an Eastern Potentate."

A half-smile seemed to play about Willard's lips. He suddenly reminded Aird of Mr. Appleton, the eighth-grade teacher, who first introduced him to algebra.

"It isn't quite that way. There are some good things written that you should read—expositions on the nature of God. I think perhaps we—the clergy—have tried to oversimplify God to the laity. It's no wonder that you are confused," said Willard.

"Can you tell us something about your church program? What do you have for the young, for instance?" It was Marion's question.

"Oh, we have the usual stuff—B.Y.F. for the kids, the women have their circles. We have tried for a men's fellowship, but it hasn't really gotten off the ground."

"How successful are your programs? I mean other than your men's fellowship?"

"I guess you could say we were par for the course." He pursed his lips as he said this, and his face took on a slight frown. "For these things to really work, the people of the church—the members—have to take hold and do things. They can't expect the minister to carry the load. After all, it's their own families who are reaping the benefits of these programs, so they should have an interest in making them work."

"That's true," agreed Marion, "but somehow it seems if church programs are to work, there has to be strong leadership and direction from the pastoral staff."

"Yes, well, in the case of our church here, we are sadly lacking in staff. We don't have an associate minister or a youth director. And at the present time I'm looking for a secretary. Really, I'm trying to run a one-man show right now; not by choice, I assure you."

There were more questions and answers. Yes, he believed in open membership. Yes, the "Back Door" as described by Aird sounded interesting and would not be objectionable to him. He had often thought of starting a coffeehouse for young people in one of his churches. Yes, he would be willing to see Dick and Dar if they were to visit his church on a pulpit call. The visit ended with his wishing the committee good luck in its search.

Dorothy and Gil, who had been very quiet all through the interview, spoke up once the foursome was in the car and on the way back home.

"Well, one thing's for sure," said Gil. "The other two ministers that were visited may have been conservatives, but this one was obviously a liberal."

"A tired liberal," observed Dorothy.

"What does that mean?"

"Didn't it seem to all of you that he was awfully glad to see us leave? It was almost as though we were interrupting his afternoon siesta."

At the next pulpit committee meeting, it was agreed that Willard seemed to be lacking in enthusiasm. Alice was inclined to think that this might be the result of the difficulties he was experiencing with his congregation and the former minister. Aird wanted to agree and did so. His preaching was very impressive, and it was easy to look for reasons for his apparent faults. "But what about his wife?" Marion asked. "Why didn't he introduce us to her?" Nobody knew. They hadn't thought about that. Finally, it was agreed that Dick and Dar would visit Willard. "You can depend on it. We'll meet his wife," Dick said.

But they didn't.

"I can't understand it," said Dar when he and Dick reported back. "He just didn't seem to want us to meet his wife."

"That's right," butted in Dick. "We very pointedly told him that we would like to meet and talk to his wife, but he just told us that she had to get home and make lunch for the kids. And I guess that was that."

"But we did get a chance to see his office that the rest of you missed."

"Oh, listen to this. This is great. Go ahead, Dar," Dick laughed as he lived over the experience.

"Well, it wasn't a big office to begin with. I can see why he didn't invite the four of you to interview him there, but even with the two of us, there just wasn't anywhere to sit down."

"No kidding," said Dick. "Dar's not exaggerating. There just wasn't anywhere to sit down. Every chair in the room was occupied with books. And the desk — well, there wasn't a bare spot on it. I don't think I've ever seen such a cluttered mess. You know what that guy does? He reads and he prepares sermons. And everything else about his job bores him!"

"Well, what's your decision on Mr. Willard?" Aird asked.

"As far as I'm concerned," said Dick, "if we hired Willard, we would have to hire a business manager or assistant to do the work that he found unpleasant."

"How about it, Dar?"

"Well, I agree with Dick, only I would put it a little stronger. I think that he is lazy."

"What do you think, Alice?"

Alice uncrossed her legs and sort of lifted herself up in the easy chair that she was cushioned into. "I guess I just felt sorry for Mr. Willard with his unfortunate experience with church politics."

"Marion, have you anything to add?"

"I wasn't too impressed with him. He left a lot of unanswered questions in my mind."

"O.K. It's decided. We don't want Willard. He goes in the dead file."

But there was one thing impressive about Willard — lazy or not. He was the only minister who was visited by every member of the committee and who still did not receive a call.

nine

THE COMMITTEE was without a candidate. That the church was not without patience was surprising, to say the least. It was now the latter part of November, and the search had been going on for better than three months. At the beginning the congregation had admonished the committee to take its time and do a good job, and in return had been cautioned that this might take until the beginning of the new year, a full four months away. This, it appeared, was perfectly all right. The church was willing to wait even that long for the right man. But now it was obvious to the committee that they would be lucky if they had a candidate to present to the church before spring. While there was no need yet to panic, it was an appropriate time to consider a new approach in the search for this elusive man.

When the group had first met with Dr. Worden, he had left them a handbook called *Calling a Baptist Minister* prepared by the American Baptist Convention for use by pulpit committees. At the time, the five had taken turns breezing through it, and then the handbook was filed away while they confidently went about the task of picking a minister from the sheaf of resumés given them by Dr. Worden. Now that these had all been appraised and discarded with no candidate at hand, the handbook was dug out of the file and read with greater intensity.

The handbook stated that an interim minister should be found so as to take the pressure for a quick decision off the pulpit committee. That had been done. The board of deacons had brought Rev. Robert Waite out of retirement to take over the pastoral duties of the church. He fit like a glove.

The book suggested that a letter be sent to the congregation informing them that the search might take some time, would be done in confidence, and that no information would be supplied the congregation until the committee had arrived at a decision to recommend a candidate. This also had been done. The letter which was sent out was tailored closely to the format suggested in the booklet.

But the handbook said other things, too, that had been completely ignored. These now were reread through more experienced, but humbler eyes.

Perhaps the single most important section of the handbook to the committee was the directory of state conventions, city societies, and Baptist seminaries. It was decided now that services of these agencies should be utilized in the search. Marion, as secretary of the committee, was given the assignment of writing to the city societies and seminaries in neighboring states for recommendations and suggestions.

Until this time, the only formally solicited recommendations that had been received by the committee had come from the state office. However, a number of unsolicited suggestions from well-meaning and interested friends or members of the church had been received. Strangely enough, the two women on the committee, Alice and Marion, were the ones who received most of the suggestions of this type. Marion, in particular, found this to be somewhat distressing. The security which the committee had inflicted upon itself made it impossible for her to extend even the normal social courtesy of informing the tipster just what disposition the committee had made of his candidate. This became even more disturbing to her as time went on and it became apparent that while no positive action was taking place in regard to the suggestions made by these people, the committee itself hadn't produced any other candidate for the church.

In spite of what may have been thought, careful study was given to each suggestion made. Unfortunately, most of the ministers referred to the committee in this manner needed the Cedar City church much more than the church needed them. Perhaps looking through the eyes of those who knew them well, each of these candidates had unusual abilities and talents. But as seen through the critical eyes of the committee, each was an individual with obvious weaknesses that offset whatever charm, sincerity, enthusiasm, or other qualities they had that had appealed to their sponsor. The one exception was Rev. Carl Bender. The committee decided to consider him next.

The name of Mr. Bender first came to the attention of the committee by way of a letter sent to Marion by a former member of the church. She had a man in mind who, unfortunately, was not entirely happy where he was now located, or so she felt, but who would fit in wonderfully with the Cedar City church. To the committee it seemed like the same old story. What the church needed wasn't someone who was running away from a problem, but rather a minister who would have to be enticed away from a successful and happy ministry. A half-hearted request was made to Dr. Worden's office for Mr. Bender's dossier. It arrived almost simultaneously with an answer to a letter Marion had written to the state secretary. This answer gave the names of several ministers in the state who might meet the church's needs. High on that list was the name of Carl Bender. Later, Mr. Bender was recommended to the committee by one of the seminaries, even though he was not a graduate of that school – but that came much later.

There were good reasons for Bender to be so well recommended. His dossier was outstanding in every way. He was a graduate of a Big Ten university. His seminary schooling was even more prestigious. His service record was one of steady advancement. Nothing in his resumé indicated anything but a harmonious relationship in his present post. When the pulpit committee had reviewed his resumé, they found themselves in complete accord. But, of all the committee, Dick Walker was the most enthusiastic. Bender and he were graduates of the same school. Not only that, Dick liked the way the man prepared his resumé. It was businesslike and to the point. He answered the questions thoroughly and intelligently. Arrangements were made for Dick and Dar to visit Carl Bender and his church as well as several others located nearby. Only Bender proved to be a possible candidate.

Dick and Dar decided to leave on Saturday and stay overnight. A small conflict arose in that the day of their departure was also the day of the Michigan State-Notre Dame football game, and Dick had to see his alma mater get tied by Notre Dame before leaving his television set and starting out on the road. This late start resulted in a late arrival and perhaps contributed to a couple of traumatic experiences which these two pillars of the church otherwise might not have experienced. Dick told it as part of his report at the next pulpit committee meeting following their trip, with Dar, as usual, standing by adding a word or two.

"We arrived in this town after dark, and of course were lost. I stopped at the side of the road so that Dar could look over the map and the directions that had been sent to us. I must say, we were in a seedy part of town, which was pretty well alive with the usual Saturday night festivities."

"Dick wanted me to get out of the car and ask directions at one of the shining night spots on the corner of the street where we were parked," cut in Dar. "But I wasn't getting out of that car or even unlocking the door."

"That's right," laughed Dick. "So there we sat struggling with the map, and down the street here came three of the flooziest-looking floozies that you would ever want to meet, and they walked right up to the car."

"They had their eyes on Dick," Dar added.

"I don't think so," said Dick, "but nevertheless, here they came, all three of them, and they stopped long enough to invite us to have a good time on the town, which of course we turned down."

"How could you hear what they had to say with the doors locked and the windows rolled up?"

"Well, now, I think you had better ask Dar that question. He unrolled the window."

Dar had a silly look on his face. "After all, we were strangers in town. You at least should listen to what people say when they speak to you."

"So what happened then?"

"Oh, we got out of there as quickly as we could, which was right away," Dick assured them. "However, that wasn't the end of our experiences. We finally found a motel in the general neighborhood of the church, and I tell you that wasn't easy that late on a Saturday night without reservations."

"Yeah, I almost forgot about that," Dar was laughing away to himself. "Tell them about that crazy innkeeper."

"So we went to this motel, and the clerk told us that he had only one available room and we could share it, which we agreed to do. After all, Dar doesn't snore that much. So we got the key, and what do you think? That room had one double bed! Back to the desk clerk, and Dar really told him. 'What do you think we are?' Dar says. 'You are going to have to do better than this if you expect us to stay here. We are certainly not using the bridal suite.' "

"He didn't say that?"

"Yes, he did. Didn't you, Dar?"

"Yeah, I sure did. That guy had a lot of nerve. He sure did."

"Well, we left that motel and finally found one down the strip another one-half mile."

"Well, let's forget about your romantic experiences

for a while and talk about Bender. How did things go with him?"

"Well, now," said Dick. "Let me tell you about him. He's a little fellow, puts you in mind a lot of Dr. Post — about the same height, same build. Getting a little gray at the temples. A young Dr. Post, I would say — has the same slow, easy gait. Doesn't talk too loud. In fact, if you saw him in a crowd, you probably wouldn't pay much attention to him."

"That's right. Let me tell you what I thought," Dar leaned forward in his chair. "When you saw him first in the sanctuary, it was hard to pick him out as a minister. He didn't stand out. He wasn't imposing, but when he got behind the pulpit, he looked comfortable, as though he belonged there. And during the sermon you didn't tire of him. He kept your attention."

"Was he a good preacher?" asked Marion.

"Well, now," it was Dick speaking. "Not bad. Not bad. But that wasn't what impressed me so much as the manner in which he talked, and the things he said when we met with him later. He's sort of like an old shoe. He fits well. Answers questions easily and to the point. He's not one of these 'Holy Joe' sort of guys. He gives you a good, practical, down-to-earth reply to the things you ask, which is a little surprising too, because he's an egghead, you know. Got a real education. The other thing I liked about him was his sense of humor. It would sort of sneak up on you. He'd throw a 'funny' in when you least expected it."

"Dick, tell them about the church school class."

"Yes, I was going to get to that, Dar. After church they have an adult class, which he invited us to attend. He didn't seem at all backward or timid about our being there, although, of course, we went out of our way to conceal our identity."

Dar was sitting over on the other side of the room laughing to himself again. "Oh," asked Aird, "what's so funny?"

"Well," said Dar, "when we got down there, since we were strangers, we were asked to stand and introduce ourselves. Dick got up and gave his name and said he was from a power utility company and talked for about five minutes about the Consumers Power installation in town."

"That's right. I had been down there for Consumers Power about five years ago. While I didn't say I was down for Consumers Power this time on business, I did feel that a little interjection about the Consumers plant facility would plant the seed in their minds."

"What did you say, Dar? Your softener business doesn't extend that far."

"Oh, I just got up and said that I was Darwin Wood, a friend of Dick Walker's, and sat down."

"You know," said Dick, "you should have seen that guy operate down there. I mean Bender. They had a regular Bible discussion with a lot of people expressing some pretty strong opinions. He just fielded each controversial question as it arose, not giving dogmatic answers, but by his very remarks, stimulating more questions and more interest. I think this was when he was at his very best."

"You liked him?"

"Yes, and his wife, too. She's sharp, personable, and has enough common sense to keep her mouth shut and let him talk."

"You would like to have him?"

"Well, let me put it this way. He's by far the best I have seen, and I would be happy to have him come. How about you, Dar?"

"I would have to agree. I think he'd fit in very well. He might not set the world on fire, but he'd do a real good job."

Aird sighed softly. Finally a man had been reached that at least two of the committee members were sold on. The others were equally responsive to the report. It was decided that the Larchers and Frazers would visit Bender just as quickly as a trip could be arranged.

Before the committee was to meet again, Bender had been revisited. In addition, the Frazers and Airds had made a highly significant visit to Wisconsin.

ten

IT HAD BEEN SNOWING ALL MORNING. When they started off at noon, the expressway was glazed with a film of ice. Over this a blanket of snow was forming, and the leaden sky gave no promise that the snowfall would soon end. The trip was being made in the Frazers' station wagon. Gil had estimated that by averaging a driving time of fifty miles an hour the destination in Wisconsin would be reached by seven in the evening. But sitting in the back of the wagon, feeling the rear wheels slipping and sliding, the Airds had serious doubts that they would reach their destination at all on that snowy day.

Earlier that day Aird had called the Frazers from his office. It had been snowing even harder then, and the trip seemed foolhardy. Marion had answered. Yes, she had seen the weather. No, she didn't think the trip should be postponed. "We won't find a minister sitting home looking out the window." Somehow that couldn't be argued. "Besides," she went on, "we have such a full schedule it would be quite a job to change it." This was true enough. He resigned himself to the trip, making a mental note to be sure never to get trapped into serving on a pulpit committee again.

After the first hour on the road, the temperature seemed to climb so that the snow turned to a wet slush and fewer cars were seen in ditches. By the time Gil had driven into Illinois the snow was gone, and he was driving in a drizzle of rain. This, at least, made the driving less dangerous. He stepped down on the throttle, trying to make up lost time. Dorothy opened a thermos of coffee and passed out some coffee cake.

There was a brief stop for lunch just north of Chicago, and then they were back on their way over what seemed to be an endless stretch of flat pavement.

It grew dark. During the day there had been a rotation of drivers and a variety of seating arrangements. Now, on this last leg of the journey, Gil was back behind the wheel with Aird as copilot, and Dorothy and Marion were sitting in the back.

Even during the hazardous driving at the beginning of the trip, there had been lighthearted chatter. Every trip to meet a minister seemed so much an adventure — held such promise — that optimism and good cheer were easily generated. But now, driving through the black night, the rain splashing on the windshield, a spray of water shooting off from the tires into the gloomy darkness that lay just beyond the headlight rays, there was no chatter, only quietness as four pairs of eyes checked off the exit numbers along the highway. Aird glanced over at Gil. He held the wheel easily, firmly, looking as relaxed as though sitting in his favorite chair in his living room.

"Are you awake?"

He laughed quietly. "Oh, yeah. I'm awake," he said.

"Your mind seemed far away."

"I was just thinking, those four weddings that the flower shop has to handle should be delivered by now."

"You hope," Marion chimed in from the back seat.

Aird looked closely at him. "Are you concerned?"

"O-o-oh, not really. I checked out each of the jobs pretty carefully this morning. The floral arrangements were about done even then, and I've got a pretty responsible guy who takes over when I'm gone who will make sure that the deliveries are made on schedule. Even so, with weddings you never know what might happen."

"There it is," Dorothy chimed in. "That's our exit coming up — one mile ahead, the sign says."

"Did it say anything about a place to sleep?"

"Food and motels this exit," she sang out in a "coffee, tea, or milk" voice.

Gil swung over into the exit lane and turned off the highway. Motel row was on the main drag into town. They took their choice and checked into their rooms just seven and one half hours from the time the trip had started. The snow, ice, sleet, and rain had delayed them but half an hour.

It was agreed to meet in the dining room of the motel at eight o'clock. This allowed some time to freshen up and also let Aird call the prospective candidate.

Rev. James R. Ellis had been recommended by his state Baptist convention. It was a shot in the dark. This man was earning more than First Baptist could afford to pay. Besides, he was already pastoring a church much larger than what was being offered. But something in the correspondence between the committee and Ellis had led Aird to believe that perhaps there was a possibility of reaching such a man. Somehow the man had not played up the importance of material considerations. Nevertheless, Aird couldn't help wondering anew, as he picked up the phone, if perhaps this long journey might not end up being another wasted trip.

Mr. Ellis himself answered the phone.

He did not appear to be the type of man who wasted words. He was glad they had arrived safely. No, it would not be possible for his wife and him to join the committee for dinner — his wife was at the airport picking up his daughter who was coming home from college for Christmas vacation. Why not go ahead and eat, and he would join them in the dining room for coffee in about forty-five minutes.

It was a large motel. The units that the Frazers and Airds occupied were so far back from the motel dining room that it was necessary — in the wetness of the night — to get back in the car and drive to a parking area closer to the dining room.

After they were seated, and while they were studying the menu, Marion filled the others in on the schedule. The only opportunity to appraise Mr. Ellis would be tonight. On Sunday morning his choir was presenting a Christmas cantata, and he would not be preaching. If one couple wished to visit his church anyway, that would be all right. However, it would probably be more profitable for both couples to attend the service at Rev. Russell Roe's church, who was the other candidate from this town on the committee's list. Mr. Roe's service was at ten o'clock. He had agreed to meet with the committee in his study following the service. It was agreed that the Frazers and Airds would make an initial appraisal of Ellis on the basis of the interview tonight. If he looked good enough, other members of the committee could arrange to visit his church at a later date. On Sunday all four of the committee would attend services at Roe's church and interview him after the service, as a group.

With that decision made, the four allowed themselves the luxury of complete relaxation. Dorothy and Marion, in the unique way of American women, had groomed themselves in the few minutes allowed to be fresh and bright and pleasing to look at and talk with. Observing their light chatter, the laughter, and the easy conversation going on at the table, one would have been hard put to relate these folk to the tired, dispirited group huddled together in that mud-spattered station wagon, sloshing through the rain just an hour before.

Through salad, soup, and the main course, they shared stories of other adventures—vacation trips, school days, family life. The Frazers had three children. The middle one in age, Diane, was fifteen and crippled from polio, having contacted the disease one year before the Salk vaccine was developed.

"We have a snapshot of Diane taking her first step," Marion was saying. "It was the only time she ever walked." Her voice broke and she turned her head away briefly. The words had come out unexpectedly. For a brief, unguarded moment she had laid bare her heart. Aird wanted to speak, to say something that would express the sympathy he felt, but he could not. He looked gratefully to his wife, who could listen and speak compassionately with Gil and Marion about that tragic night when their year-old baby ravaged with the fever of the dreaded disease was rushed to the hospital.

She was able to help them to move in conversation to the heartlifting description of Diane's unusual, and sometimes amusing, experiences of living an almost normal life within the framework of a chin-to-foot set of braces. They all laughed at Gil's description of Diane's struggling together with him to descend a rocky path at the Grand Canyon en route to an outdoor ladies' room.

They were on dessert when Mr. Ellis approached. His resumé had included a picture, but if they hadn't been expecting him, it's doubtful if they would have recognized him. Aird first noticed him as he entered the dining room at the far end from where the group was sitting. The hostess was pointing out the table to him, and then in what seemed about three strides he was there. His head leaned forward as though he was perpetually prepared for low doorways. His frame was gangling, yet he gave the feeling of great strength and vitality. But it was his face!

His picture had shown a docile fortyish sort of man — one who looked his age. In reality he looked older, but his nose was prominent and straight, his eyes bright and alive. He was fighting a losing battle with baldness, and his face was etched with lines. However, what stood out was that long, straight nose and those piercing, gleaming eyes.

After introductions all the way around, he pulled up a chair and sat down. "Will you join us for dessert?" No, he thought not. But he would have some coffee. He spoke easily, with no pretention.

Marion apologized for taking him away from home when his daughter had just returned from college. He assured her that this was no real bother. So ended the formalities, and the committee went right into the business at hand. They asked him the questions that had now almost become standard. How did he reconcile the vengeful, jealous God of the Old Testament with the God of love pictured in the New? How much credence should be put on the book of Genesis? That is, they started to ask him these questions, but after the first one or two, they just sat entranced and listened. He spoke easily, confidently, almost casually. Yet, his words were vibrant with color, imagination, and life. In answer to the first two questions asked, he talked about the Old Testament. He wasn't a slave to it, stuck with defending the veracity of folktales that would have insulted the intelligence and sensitivity of his listeners. But neither was he prepared to discard a book which he obviously felt was divinely inspired writing. Rather, he spoke of the Old Testament as a collection of truths wrapped in the language and customs of an ancient, oriental land. To illustrate his thinking, he took several stories from the Old Testament, unwrapped the mythology, the quaint language, the customs, and the tribal prejudices, and revealed the underlying truths.

Aird tried to place him into one of the regular classifications he had mentally established for the ministers already seen, but he wouldn't fit. He was atypical. He spoke freely—almost with abandon. There was no caution or reservation. It was like hearing a symphony of words.

They sat and talked around the dinner table, the four from Cedar City and Ellis, until it was obvious that their prolonged presence was becoming an inconvenience to the waitress. But they hadn't even begun to tell him about the church in Cedar City. Though it was late, Aird invited Ellis to visit in the motel room to talk further. He was agreeable.

They all picked up their coats at the cloakroom, but the check girl had trouble finding Ellis's. "It's a trench coat," he told her. "It's easily recognized by a torn pocket."

It was still raining when they walked from the restaurant. "I think it would be better for you to drive up to the motel unit, rather than walk in this rain," Aird said. "Why don't I join you in your car and show you the way?"

Ellis agreed. They got in his car, and he started the engine. It roared. "The muffler," he explained, "blew last week, and I haven't had a chance to fix it."

The Airds' room was double size, and it had been decided to continue the discussion there. Gil Frazer brought in a couple of chairs from his room, and the conversation started again where it had left off in the dining room.

Marion brought out a brochure of Cedar City and an annual report of the church and handed them to Ellis to look at. He looked at them casually, almost disinterestedly. He fumbled in his pocket for a moment and brought out a packet of cigarettes. "Do you mind if I smoke?" Aird had his first pang of disappointment, but he dismissed it abruptly. After all, it was a personal, not a religious, matter.

"We have this thing called 'The Back Door,' " he said. "It's located on the lower level of the Christian education building and it's called 'The Back Door' because the entrance is off the alley at the back of the building."

"Is it a coffeehouse?"

"It started off that way — with folk singers and all, but it's now really a teen-age dance hall. There are still the little coffee tables and the kids can buy coffee or soft drinks, but the big attraction is the dancing and the bands. The bands are usually rock and roll outfits from around town — high school groups."

"Do you have a good attendance — do many of your own young people attend?"

"Well," Marion studied the wall over his head for a moment. "No, very few of our own children attend. There is good attendance — usually two hundred kids or more, wouldn't you say, Gil?"

Gil agreed. "Yes, I would say so. Most of them have no church affiliation at all. In fact, we've got some pretty rough kids among that crowd."

"Let's put it bluntly, Gil. They don't come much tougher. We have a policeman on duty at all times. A police patrol car checks in at least once a night. Usually at least one teen-ager has to be thrown out for drinking. At that last dance I chaperoned I overheard one sweet little fifteen-year-old say to another, 'I hope we can get by that crowd of guys outside the back door without getting raped.' " Aird looked directly at Ellis. "Sometimes we wonder if perhaps we shouldn't be spending our time and money on our own kids."

Ellis looked at Aird steadily, and a smile drifted across his face. "What makes you so sure that these aren't your own kids? You're a downtown church. Don't you think your outreach should go beyond the children of your church members or those you get into Sunday school? Is your church ministry to be restricted to the kids who will come to a Saturday night Bible discussion or play parlor games in the church basement? Do you think Christ's ministry was restricted in such a way to his friends only?"

His cigarette lay burning in the ash tray by his side while he spoke. Now he picked it up, took a couple of quick puffs, snuffed it out, and lit another one. "What kind of success do you have with your young people's programs, by the way?"

It was Marion who answered. "Wel-l-l-l, not much, I'm afraid."

"And what's wrong?"

"We really don't know. We do well with the elementary school years and even junior high school. But once the kids reach senior high level, they seem to lose interest in our program."

He nodded. "You're not alone. All kinds of churches are having the same problem. Our church youth programs are just not reaching the kids. We're not up to date. We are not with it. We are so busy putting across our stereotyped program that we don't have time to communicate with the kids on their own level. Consequently, in my church we never feel compelled to get into our prepared program. Sometimes we never get beyond the coke machine. Some youngster will ask a question that is bothering him, and we end up with a bull session right there that takes us through the entire period."

Aird asked him his standard question on the racial matter.

Ellis leaned back, slipped off his glasses, and rubbed his huge nose. "What should I say? No minister worthy of his calling dare say that he would refuse fellowship to any Christian, regardless of his color. But then, if he wants to keep Negroes out, he doesn't have to. All he has to do is do nothing, and no matter how many holy, sanctimonious, pious platitudes he mouths about the equality of man, no Negro will penetrate the invisible wall surrounding his respectable white church. No, I must say even more. The Negro's problem relates to the social, the economic, the educational, the spiritual spheres of life. It is the duty of the church – particularly your church in its downtown location – to stand by the Negro, to help him in his struggle to get out into fresh air, to breathe, to live. You can do this in the name of Christianity, but if not, then do it in the name of self-preservation, because the Negro is not going to stay down much longer. If he doesn't make it with our help, he will make it without it – and the ensuing struggle will not be pretty to see."

They weren't getting comforting answers, but they kept right on asking. Ellis's ash tray contained a mound of butts when Marion finally asked the question she saved for the close of all interviews.

"Reverend Ellis, considering your present situation here, are there circumstances that, ah, indicate that your present environment is not compatible with your outlook? What I would like to say is, there must be some rather extenuating reasons for you to consider a move from such a stimulating area to Cedar City."

He snuffed out his last cigarette of the evening.

"Have you seen my church? No? Even if your plans won't let you attend services tomorrow, you ought to at least drive by. We moved into it three years ago. It's very large and very beautiful and very rich." He said it dispassionately, like a guide on a museum tour. "We have several millionaires in that church, and many more right on the fringe of making it. Our wealth scares people away. Young couples are timid about joining. Our building is located in a fine suburb, well-insulated from the city proper and all its problems. Our people like it that way. They don't want to know, and they don't want to be involved — not only that, but they don't want their minister to get involved either."

For a moment there was silence in the room, then Aird spoke. "Our situation is much different, of course. We're located right in the center of town — we can't help but be involved. However, we are different, too, in that I don't think we have one millionaire. Our expense budget is much less than that of your church. The financial renumeration probably would not match what you are receiving or can anticipate for the future from your church."

Ellis turned slightly to look at Aird squarely. "Jack, if I thought I could best serve there, I'd accept a call to a ghetto church." It was said quietly, simply, without bravado. Aird believed he would and asked if he would be willing to talk with the other members of the pulpit committee and have them visit his church. He said he would. Marion said she would be in contact with him. Dorothy retrieved his torn coat from the coat closet, and the committee saw him to the door. It was 12:30 A.M. The rain had stopped. When he started the engine of his car, the muffler seemed louder than ever. He rolled down the window and hollered out. "I'll try and make a quick getaway before your neighbors can know what awakened them." They all laughed.

It was the last time they ever saw him.

At breakfast the next morning the coffee was cold, and the pancakes were soggy, but it didn't matter much. Their minds weren't on food. It was even difficult to concentrate on Roe, who was the object of the day.

"I wish Ellis didn't smoke," Aird said half apologetically, expecting to be trampled. He was.

"Oh, I don't think that means a thing," exclaimed Dorothy. "After all, that's his own personal business."

"I agree with Dorothy," said Marion. "After all, Dr. Post smoked a pipe. I don't think anyone ever complained about that."

"You're sold on this man?" Aird asked.

Gil laughed. "Aren't we all?" Aird couldn't help but smile. Though he felt that the pulpit committee trips were a husband-and-wife team effort, both Gil and Dorothy went out of their way to emphasize that they were not on the committee and were not taking an active part. "Our purpose here is to chaperon," Gil would say. While they were present during the interviews, it was seldom that either asked a question or made a comment. Later, however, when evaluating the candidate, they could be depended upon to voice a strong position for or against. There was no doubt that they were both competely sold on Ellis. The night before, when the lights were off and they were settled in bed, Aird and Dorothy had reviewed together the meeting with Ellis. Her last words as she was drifting off to sleep were, "I think you have found your man." He remembered, in a semi-conscious state, mumbling, "We visit Roe tomorrow – let's give him a fair chance."

There's always the problem of parking the car. When you have an out-of-state license, do you brazenly drive right into the church parking lot, or park across the street from the entrance where everyone can wonder why you are hiding your car? Probably they were overly sensitive on this score. Surely, most churches have out-of-town visitors who are not there for the purpose of stealing the congregation's minister. In any case, if the church visited has a large attendance, the question is academic since at the time of a visitor's arrival – five minutes before the opening hymn – the parking spaces near the church are usually filled. This wasn't the case at Roe's church, however. There was ample choice of parking places and likewise ample choice of pews.

Mr. Roe's church was an old church. It was dying with the neighborhood. The choir tried manfully to conquer a selection it should have surrendered to years before. The usual hymns were sung by the congregation in an anemic fashion. Roe himself was a good-looking man – even handsome. Rather short in height, he was straight and trim with broad, athletic shoulders that tapered down to a slim waist. When he spoke, his voice was pleasant to listen to. The substance of his sermon, while not exciting or provocative, was at least reasonable and in keeping with basic Baptist beliefs.

When the service had finally ended, the Frazers and Airds, trying to stay as close to the back of the departing group as they could, slowly meandered to the door where he was shaking hands. It was the same old routine, and they were no more successful than usual. They seemed to be surrounded by people when they reached Roe. At the mention of names, he flickered not an eyelid. After shaking hands, the committee walked off as inconspicuously as possible to the side entrance of the church and waited there for him to complete his salutations to the last few remaining parishioners. It was too cold to wait outside but waiting inside was awkward. Those of the congregation leaving by the side exit seemed to stare as they walked by. Aird assured himself that this would be the last time he took part in a candidate interview at a church office. In the future, all such interviews would either be done the previous night or at least in a neutral place far away from the local parishioners.

Eventually, the last of the lingerers left, and Roe guided them into his office. It was a large room sparsely furnished with a large, bare, wooden desk in the middle of the room. On the far wall was an electric clock. It read 1:25. Gil instinctively looked at his watch. Mr. Roe caught him in the act. "Don't be alarmed about the time," he said. "We went off Daylight Saving Time last September, and the custodian just hasn't gotten around to set back the clock."

Gil laughed. "It will be a long enough ride home without losing an hour before we even get started."

During the next hour they asked Roe all the questions in their repertoire, and he answered them straightforwardly and candidly. He was easy to talk to and easy to like. After a while his wife joined the group and took part in a general discussion about the problems relating to maintaining an inspiring young people's program.

The Roes had a large family of children, and, though nothing was said, Dorothy and Marion were getting concerned that the interview was delaying their dinner. The committee cut off conversation a little earlier than otherwise they might have done and bade the Roes good-bye.

In the car Gil was the first to speak. "He wants the job," he said.

Dorothy added, "With all those kids he probably needs the job. I doubt if his present church pays him enough to live on."

"He sure is handsome."

"Oh, come on, Marion. In five years he's liable to be fat and bald."

"Let's just take one year at a time." They all laughed. It had a relaxing effect. The subject was Roe, but they were thinking about Ellis. Finally Gil voiced what was on all their minds.

"Let's stop the car and call Ellis and give him the job right now."

"I second the motion." This from Dorothy.

Marion laughed nervously. "He sure looks like he might be the one."

Gil peered into the rearview mirror. "How about you, Jack? We haven't heard anything out of you. What's your thinking on him?"

"He disturbs me – frightens me."

"Frightens you!"

"Well, maybe that's putting it a little dramatically, but I really mean that he causes me concern."

"How do you mean?"

"He's provocative. He arouses the senses and emotions. Some speakers have the ability to arouse the mind; others can arouse emotions. I think this man will do both. After listening to him, you will want to act."

"Is that bad?"

"It's dangerous. There will be conflict in the church, in the community. In fact, before he's in Cedar City for very long, the whole city would be in a turmoil."

"Why?"

"Because he truly believes that the teachings of Jesus should be taken literally. We can live with the fundamentalists who insist on literal acceptance of the story of Adam and Eve and the apple. You can accept all that or reject it with no harm done. But the conservatives — or fundamentalists — or whatever you want to call them — are careful not to preach literal acceptance of the teachings of Jesus. How would we justify our wars, particularly the one we are in now, if we took literally Jesus' admonishment to do good to those who would harm us? To turn our cheek to receive a second blow? To give the man who takes our coat our pants also? How would we justify our segregated churches, or our ghettos, when Jesus teaches love and brotherhood? At the moment, I can't think of a more unlikely and disturbing minister for our church than Ellis, unless it was Jesus Christ himself. But I have to agree with you, I would be thrilled to have him come. It would be an experience that I wouldn't want to miss."

Dorothy had been sitting quietly through all of this. Now she spoke up. What she said was in almost a whisper. "I think you're underselling our people. All of these problems have to be met, and we will meet them. All we need is a leader, someone who can prepare us for what is coming and what we should do — can do. I think Ellis might just be that man."

They were back on the highway headed south. Gil had the car purring along at the maximum allowed. Aird leaned back. For a time there was no sound but the muffled whine of the tires against the pavement.

Another visit was over. For the first time, he was bringing something back with him.

eleven

WHEN THE PULPIT COMMITTEE NEXT MET, they were faced with a pleasant dilemma. Where just a short month ago, they had no candidate considered suitable, they now were faced with two men, both of whom seemed well qualified for the First Baptist Church. Since the last meeting of the committee, in addition to the Frazers and Airds visiting Wisconsin, the Larchers and Frazers had made a follow-up visit to Ohio to the church of Rev. Carl Bender. Both Alice and Marion shared the enthusiasm exhibited by Dar Wood and Dick Walker after their contact with Bender. Alice, though, had a reservation and expressed it at the meeting.

"The thing that immediately struck me when I saw Reverend Bender behind the pulpit was his very close resemblance to our late Dr. Post."

"Well, yes, that's what Dar talked about after our visit."

"That's right, Dick, and we were prepared for a physical resemblance, but it goes much deeper than that. He resembles him in mannerism, in voice, and as far as I could make out, even in thinking, and I wouldn't be surprised if they were very close theologically. As you know, I was on the pulpit committee that called Dr. Post seventeen years ago, which would put him at that time just about the same age as Mr. Bender is now, and I had the haunting feeling that I was looking at Frank up there on the platform. It was a strange sensation, and I am afraid that it is a sensation that would be shared by many in our church if he were to become our minister."

"You think it would be a real problem?"

Alice leaned forward and pursed her lips in a characteristic manner that she had when making a definite point. "I think no matter who comes, he will be measured against our former pastor. It's just human nature. But most of the candidates will be able to assert their own personality within a few months. But Mr. Bender, he may never be able to establish his personality because of the memory of Dr. Post."

"Marion, what did you think of Bender?"

"I like him. I, too, noticed the similarity to Dr. Post, but somehow I don't feel that this is as significant as Alice does. Though when she mentioned it to me, I could see her reason for thinking so."

"Would you like to have him as a minister?" Aird asked.

"Well, I think I would like to know more about him."

"How would you compare him with Ellis?" he pressed.

Marion frowned. She wasn't ready to make such a comparison yet. "You have to remember that when Alice and I visited Bender, we only attended his morning church service. We didn't have an opportunity to talk personally with him or his wife."

"But even so, you must have drawn some comparison," insisted Dick.

Marion set her lips firmly. "Well, yes, if I must make a choice, I would have to go along with Mr. Ellis."

Aird watched Dick closely. He knew Dick was completely sold on Bender and for a minute thought he saw a frown cross his face. But if so, Dick hid it quickly. "Well, I must say, this fellow Ellis must be pretty all right."

"Enough so, Dick," Aird interjected, "that we would recommend that you, Dar, and Alice take the long trip up there to visit him right after the holidays. Meanwhile, I would like to visit Bender because from everything I have heard from the rest of your reports, he's a first-class candidate."

"That's right," said Dick. "I like that idea. It will give us a good comparison."

The meeting ended in a lighthearted note. The committee had two very promising candidates. They would take the two-week break for Christmas and New Year's with the comfortable feeling that at long last they were nearing the point of decision. Marion would correspond with both men and set up visits for the first week-end after New Year's Day.

Both Ellis and Bender answered Marion's letters promptly, agreeing to the proposed visits. Once their replies were received, the holidays were no longer a rest from the search, but rather a delay — an obstacle — to the completion of this job that each member of the committee so badly wanted to finish.

While they waited, the committee unashamedly ferreted out every bit of information they could obtain on each of the men. Marion contacted schools, ministerial associations, former pastoral associations, former parishioners, and the state office. The information she received was almost uniformly positive.

Both were well educated, with perhaps Bender having the edge. Both had a background of fine experience, with Ellis perhaps showing the more oustanding results. Ellis, at the present time, had reached the higher pinnacle of success when measured against the size and status of the church now being served. It was on this score that the committee had a concern about Ellis. Why should a man, in the peak years of his career, be willing to leave a church that quite obviously was better prepared to reward his efforts more fully than was the Cedar City church? Even considering his apparent zeal for helping the downtrodden, it seemed that his present church's budget allowed more leeway for activity in this area of work than the relatively small Cedar City budget. The answer to this came back. Within Dr. Ellis's congregation were many people who were less than enthusiastic about his civil rights and inner-city activities. Not only did they show their displeasure by their attitudes in church, but he and his family were being plagued by crank letters and telephone calls. Knowing this didn't discourage the Cedar City committee in the least. Rather, in helping to explain his willingness to leave his present church, it made his candidacy more promising than ever. It was exciting to think that a man who had proven his desire to work in these areas would consider Cedar City. Dick and Dar waited impatiently for the first weekend in the new year to visit this very unusual and dedicated man.

The phone rang. "Dad, it's for you." It was a Sunday night — New Year's Day. Aird roused himself from his easy chair and headed for the phone. He had just returned from driving his daughter back to Blissfield College and wondered what she had forgotten to take back with her this time. "By the way, Mrs. Larcher called while you were gone. Said she would call back tomorrow." He wondered what Alice might have wanted.

"Hello." It was Dick Walker's voice. "Jack, what do you think of that? Isn't it a horrible thing?"

"What are you talking about, Dick?"

"Haven't you heard? Didn't Marion call?"

"No. But I had a call from Alice Larcher while I was out. Dick, what is it?"

"Well, that figures. Mrs. Larcher would want to call you herself." (He was still calling Alice "Mrs. Larcher" even after five months of committee work together.)

"Dick, when are you going to tell me what's wrong?"

"Reverend Ellis shot himself!"

"He shot himself?"

"That's right. They found him slumped over his desk in the church office. I don't know any more than that. In fact, I wouldn't have called you at all if I hadn't thought you had already received the information from either Marion or Mrs. Larcher. She, that is Mrs. Larcher, got the information someplace. I don't know how, but. . . ."

He talked on, but Aird hardly heard what he said. When he put down the phone, he walked slowly back into the living room and sank down into his easy chair, only vaguely aware that his wife was standing by waiting to hear about the telephone conversation. He had a vague, deep-seated uneasiness that he couldn't understand. He could see Mr. Ellis once again sitting with the group, driving home his point, and it was his eyes he remembered most. They sparkled — gleamed. They had a sharpness, a bright, alert sharpness. He hadn't seen Ellis angry, but his eyes had given promise of being able to pierce and stab flashing anger with the same exuberance that they showed in laughter. Even when sprawled out on a motel chair much too small for his long, lanky frame, he had exuded vitality, strength, a zest and zeal for living. And now this man with those flashing eyes, whose every gesture and vocal expression seemed to express dynamic life, whose love of people and living was evident in everything they had heard him say, had shot himself.

When he had recounted the telephone conversation to Dorothy, her reaction was one of sympathy and concern for the man's wife, and what the sudden shock must mean to her. Aird, listening to her talk, realized that this deep, vague uneasiness that he had felt did not relate to sympathy. Up until now, he hadn't thought about Ellis's wife and family and what this must mean to them, and he was ashamed that he had not. But his feelings were for something else, and it bothered him that he really didn't know just what it was that was upsetting him so. He reviewed in his mind once again the trip to Wisconsin and the visit with Ellis, feeling again the thrill and the challenge of the thoughts expressed by the man. Then suddenly he felt a sharp resentment that a man who had the capability of affecting him in this way should then kill himself, and Aird began to realize just why he had this uneasiness — this vague, empty uneasiness that was bothering him.

For four months the committee had been searching for a minister. During that time, they had had several disappointments. They had learned that much of their thinking when they started required modification and that many of their preconceived ideas had to be discarded. The one thing that had remained unchanged was their confidence, their optimism. They had an almost fatalistic feeling that eventually they would find the right man. Aird had felt in himself and in the others, though it was never discussed, a confidence in their ability to interpret just what the church needed and wanted. He had interviewed and evaluated candidates without question in his own mind but had felt that the decisions he had helped make were correct. Now, after turning down the candidacies of several dozen men, the one minister who he had felt was completely qualified and who undoubtedly would have received his support in a call to the First Baptist Church of Cedar City had committed suicide. That one quick act, Aird realized, had shattered his confidence. How qualified was he to judge who was best suited to minister to and guide the lives of the six hundred people in the Cedar City church when this man, whom he had so favorably evaluated less than a month ago, had been so emotionally unbalanced in his own life that he would do such an act? What bothered Aird most was that he felt, even yet, that Ellis, as he had last seen and talked with him, was the man he would have wanted to have as pastor of his church.

twelve

ON JANUARY EIGHTH, the Airds visited Bender. The Frazers, who on their first visit to Ohio had attended Sunday morning services at Bender's church but had not had the opportunity to interview him, went also.

When they had checked into the motel on Saturday night, Aird called Carl Bender and arranged for him and his wife to come to the motel for dinner.

The motel seemed like a discreet place to eat. However, as a further security measure, it was arranged that a table for six be set up in the far corner of the room where the group could talk with a minimum of interference.

The four arrived at the restaurant first, but had hardly been seated when Mr. Bender and his wife approached. Gil and Aird rose to meet them. So did the people seated at the next table! It was only after introductions all around that Aird discovered that he had picked a table next to that occupied by four of the main pillars of Bender's church. The dinner-table conversation never got beyond weather, traffic conditions, and how the local school millage was to be met.

Later on, the Benders met with the committee members in the motel, and Aird had his first real opportunity to observe the candidate liked so well by the rest of the committee. Alice had been right. Bender looked like Dr. Post. He acted like him. Even his speaking mannerisms were the same. But at that point, it seemed to Aird, the similarity ended. Bender appeared to be a modifier. He saw both sides of every question asked. He struck a balance on every issue. He might make an ideal panel moderator — but, sitting on a white charger, he would look a little silly. Nevertheless, he was everything the others had said. Maybe the church didn't need a white knight. Aird asked of his interest in the Cedar City church and what the next step might be in the further consideration of his candidacy.

Yes, he was interested. He felt that a visit to Cedar City would be appropriate. He and his wife would arrive on a Thursday evening. They would like to visit the town, see the church, parsonage, spend whatever time was necessary with the pulpit committee to talk in more detail about material concerns, and then return home Saturday afternoon so as not to interfere with his Sunday services. It was agreed then that the pulpit committee would meet to consider inviting Rev. Carl Bender and his wife to visit Cedar City with the understanding that neither party would be obligated.

The next morning the Frazers and Airds attended the service at Bender's church. He lived up to their expectations.

As usual, on the trip home they reviewed the weekend. Carl Bender would do a good job, perhaps an exceptional job, but somehow he lacked the fire, the drive, that had been evident in Ellis.

On the following Tuesday the pulpit committee met once again. There was no doubt in anyone's mind that Bender was the best prospect yet seen. Somehow though, he just didn't invoke the image of a take-charge, inspirational-type leader that Aird had envisioned. He was just too much of a compromise. This was only a vague feeling, however, on his part. Certainly, the choice was unanimous that Bender should be invited to Cedar City for a visit. Once that decision was made, a weight seemed to lift, and the committee energetically and lightheartedly entered into the task of preparing for the event. First, the committee found that it was surprising how few Saturdays there were that were not committed either for some member of the committee or for the Benders. A date for the latter part of February was finally agreed upon. Hotel accommodations were made. An itinerary for the two days which made valuable use of every minute was established and then the committee sat back and waited.

The committee had intended during this time of waiting to continue the search, for after all, they had no assurance that Bender was their man. The leads the committee had, however, just seemed to disappear. Once the invitation had been made to Bender, they were able to generate no interest or enthusiasm in any other candidate and finally gave in to the realization that they had settled on one man, and one man alone. This only added to the excitement and tension as the date of his visit drew closer.

Since Dick Walker had been the first to meet the

Benders, it seemed right that he should act as their host and guide during their stay in Cedar City. He met them at their hotel on Friday morning and squired them about town, showing the highlights — the schools, the community college, the parks, the residential areas, downtown with its new mall, and then, finally, the parsonage. He was joined there by Marion and Harry Young, of the board of trustees, who was chairman of the grounds and facilities committee.

Up until this point, Dick had been heartened by the reaction of the Benders to the city. They were impressed by the beautiful parkway, even in the dreary month of February. The large number of top-rate golf courses had meant very little to Bender, but he had perked up considerably when Dick had pointed out the numerous small lakes dotting the perimeter of town. Mrs. Bender, a schoolteacher and a mother of several school-age children, was particularly interested in the schools and impressed by the new Central High School, which served the district in which the parsonage was located. The reaction was decidedly different when they entered the parsonage.

The parsonage held a special place in the hearts of the congregation. The chairman of the board of trustees had been married in its parlor in 1929. When visited by the laity of the church, the parsonage brought back nostalgic memories of a type of life unknown to the modern age. No built-in kitchen here! The living room was a model of an old-time parsonage parlor. A stairway leading up from the living room made accessible three bedrooms with a minimum of ventilation. The bathroom, also on the upstairs floor, was adorned with a bathtub setting on steel legs. As a further concession to hygiene, in one corner of the basement was a spray nozzle over a drain for taking a standup shower. The old coal furnace loomed large. Marion, Dick, and Harry Young showed the place to the best possible advantage, assuring Mrs. Bender that something could be done about "that kitchen" and that naturally "remodeling would be done to suit her taste." Later, when Dick reported back to the committee, he said, "I don't think they were impressed."

Following the visit to the parsonage, Marion and Dick took the Benders to lunch, where Aird joined them. After lunch they all went to the church to see the building.

The First Baptist Church has stood on the corner of Elm and Main for 125 years. It is a majestic structure, built of dark red brick with a high spire that can be seen all over the downtown area of town. The ivy on the brick only adds to its distinction as a proud, old landmark. The sanctuary seats about seven hundred people with a small balcony at the rear. The ceiling is high and the acoustics have a quality not often found in buildings built today. The appointments of the sanctuary have been well maintained. It is a bright, gracious place to worship. Adjoining the church is an educational building, built in recent years, which includes excellent facilities for religious education classes and activities. Also in this building is the pastor's study, which is spacious and bright and easy to work in. All in all, it is a facility that the people of Cedar City are, and have the right to be, very proud of. The Benders, this time, were impressed. They lingered a long time looking the place over and asking questions. It was obvious that this was a facility that the Benders would enjoy working in, and Dick, who had been dejected after the visit to the parsonage, now took renewed heart.

After everything had been seen and all the questions had been asked, by prearranged plans Marion Frazer and Dorothy Aird, who had joined the group, took Mrs. Bender on a shopping tour of downtown Cedar City, while Dick and Aird sat down with Mr. Bender in the pastor's study to discuss some of the business matters involved in hiring a minister.

They were prepared for some financial negotiation. After all, even a minister and his family have to eat, and in spite of careful phrasing of words most ministers interviewed readily made it known that while they were not in the work to get rich, they did have a responsibility to themselves to obtain the best salary the situation would allow. Bender expressed it rather pointedly and accurately as he explained, "I feel that when a person makes a move he should, if he is worth his salt, expect to move at an increase in salary. Also, that increase should be substantial because it has been my experience that the easiest time to get a church to consider a salary increase is on an occasion like this. Once the minister is in, the congregation has a tendency to take him for granted. His financial needs are the very last considered in the preparation of a budget and the very first cut when a budget is not met." Looking back over their church's own recent history, Aird could find no fault with this remark and told him the maximum salary that the church was prepared to pay. This, it appeared, was satisfactory. Aird settled back rather relieved. The worst was over. But Bender had more to say. "I think we ought to discuss just what you might expect of me in the way of time if I were to be your minister." The large round-rimmed glasses on his round, full face gave him an almost owlish appearance. "You see, I have a philosophy about this work — that a minister can only give so much, and then he will find himself drained spiritually, emotionally, and physically." Dick and Aird nodded their heads in agreement.

"I feel quite strongly that it is necessary for a minister to get away a couple of weeks a year and attend workshops or seminars, which will feed him, replenish him, perhaps even give him new insight, so that he can continue to do a good job and keep up with the changing times."

"Just what kind of workshop or seminar would you be talking about?" Dick asked.

"Well, there is quite a famous one in Michigan at Bloomfield Hills, and then there are similar things put on by some of the leading eastern universities. There might be some years when the one that would be appropriate to me would last quite a few days, perhaps it may last several weeks. But I feel very strongly that in my next charge there must be a prior agreement with the board of deacons that I be allowed such freedom, for certainly I am convinced that the main benefactor will be the church."

"Well," Dick said, "while we can't speak for the board of deacons, we probably could sell this idea without too much trouble. After all, I guess we could do without a minister for that short period, particularly when we stand to benefit from it."

"There is something else," Bender continued. "Possibly I can forget about it and iron it out after I get here. But I want to be completely fair with you and make sure that everything is above board and understood prior to a final decision being made." Aird glanced over to Dick and, for the first time, noted a sign of apprehension on his face.

"You see, we have this summer home in New York. It isn't a pretentious place, but it's the only home we have that's really our own. It's on a lake there, and Isabella, my wife, and the children go there for the summer when the school year is completed."

"Do you expect that your wife will be teaching if you come to Cedar City?"

"Yes, we have discussed this, and it would seem that in order to put aside the money required for educational purposes for the children, it will be necessary for her to continue teaching. The two and one-half months in the summer is her opportunity to relax and rest up for the coming year."

"Don't you find that it is a little difficult to be alone for such a long period of time?"

"Well, not really. First of all, of course, one month of that time is my vacation, and I join them up there. We try to work it so that I take my vacation for the month of August. I bring the family back in time to start school right after Labor Day. Then during the other six weeks I find an opportunity to catch up on my reading and do a lot of church business that doesn't normally get done. As a matter of fact, it's the busiest six weeks of the year for me. I find that I put things aside during the year for this very purpose. But another thing, I do find it necessary to open the place up, and it does take, from here at least, a very full day's driving to get there. So it is possible, in fact, very probable, that I would need perhaps one-half week in June to get away and open up the cottage. Naturally, this would be planned between Monday and Saturday, so I would not be gone from the church on Sunday."

"Well, let's see now." Dick raised his eyes to heaven and started to add. "There are four weeks for vacation, two weeks for seminars, one-half week to open the cottage. That's more than six weeks, and then I suppose you intend to go to the conventions?"

"Well, yes. I think that is beneficial to the church to be represented at the state and national conventions, and in all probability I will attend most of them."

"Well, then, that adds another week and brings us to seven and one-half weeks of the year during which the church would be without your service." There was a moment's silence before Aird finally broke in.

"We appreciate your frankness in all of this, Reverend Bender. You must understand that we are not prepared to assure you now that this amount of time would be allowed, though I can guarantee you that if, and when, a call is made to you, prior approval will have been obtained from the necessary boards, giving concurrence for such an agreement. Now, let's talk for a few minutes about other pertinent matters."

The rest of the discussion was easy. He found no fault with the program of the church nor with those things which particularly were pertinent to him in his ministry. By the time Marion, Dorothy, and Mrs. Bender had returned from their shopping trip, the men had completed their discussion. Dick drove Bender and his wife back to the motel, and the rest left to prepare for the headline event of the weekend – a dinner with the full pulpit committee, followed by a final pastoral interview with the whole pulpit committee taking part.

No corporation ever worked harder or made more painstaking plans in the preparation for the interviewing of a company president than the pulpit committee did for this final session with Bender. Every aspect of the evening had been worked out in detail.

It had been decided well in advance that the dinner would be held in the Airds' home. The committee members and their spouses arrived promptly at 6:45 P.M., with the exception of Gil Frazer, who had arranged to pick up the Benders at their motel. When Gil shepherded them into the house at seven o'clock sharp, everything was ready.

The strategy was to have a cocktail hour — non-alcoholic, of course — of just that period of time to allow a complete relaxation of the candidate and his wife before sitting down to the dinner table. The group that sat down in the dining room at eight was reasonably relaxed and certainly good-humored.

In line with the overall staff strategy, Dorothy Aird had prepared a beef fondue meal, the recipe of which had been acquired during several years' residence in Switzerland. The advantage of this do-it-yourself type of meal is that the meat, cooked in individual fondue pots at the table, would be a conversation prompter and thereby encourage the generally, relaxed tone that the committee wished to achieve. Looking back on it later, all agreed that the meal was a great success. In order to allow everyone to reach the fondue pots, two tables were set up, Mr. Bender at one and Mrs. Bender at the other. Mindful of Alice Larcher's comments that at the dinner interview for Dr. Post seventeen years ago all the men sat with Dr. Post and the women sat with his wife, the seating was arranged so that the two women members of the committee were at the same table as Bender. By the time the meal was over, the committee was on a "Carl and Isabelle" relationship with the Benders, and it appeared that the mission was accomplished: The committee had found their man.

The after-dinner interview seemed like a mere formality. Nevertheless, it had to be done. Dorothy invited Carl and his wife back into the living room in front of the fireplace, where she seated them on the sofa surrounded by the five members of the committee. The wives and husbands of the committee discreetly faded away, or at least, that was the plan. As it turned out, they had a little party in the kitchen all to themselves. The sounds of their laughter not only distracted those in the living room, but made the interview seem a little dull by comparison. It finally took Alice Larcher to break through and ask a penetrating and provoking question.

"Mr. Bender," she asked, "how do you feel that you would fit in with our state Baptist convention, theologically speaking?"

The candidate stared thoughtfully at the floor for a moment, mulling over this question in his mind. Undoubtedly, it was one that he had asked himself before even considering the invitation to visit Cedar City, and Aird guessed that his hesitancy was not due to striving for an answer to the question, but rather to an attempt to find the words to phrase the conclusion that he had already reached. Finally he looked up.

"I don't think, personally, that there will be any conflict between my colleagues and me in this state convention nor with the state office. I recognize, however, that my brand of theology is quite a bit more liberal than most in the state. Perhaps with the exception of one or two churches, my feeling on this subject might be considered a little more progressive — I hope that's a fair term — than most of the churches in this state convention."

"Do you mean, Reverend Bender," asked Marion, "that you would find it difficult to cooperate or participate in organized state activities? I am referring particularly to the youth work, the joint meetings, and rallies they have for young people."

"Oh, no. No, I don't say that at all. I do say, however, that it seems to me that their programs, as now set up, have very little real meaning or lasting effect on our young people, and I would be much more interested in finding more constructive, visionary, and outreaching programs than those now offered by the state convention."

Aird glanced around the room. Alice was nodding in agreement; Marion looked worried. Dar had no look at all, a mask that he often put on when he was still groping for a position or answer. Dick was smiling. Aird was sure that in his mind Dick was neither agreeing nor disagreeing but finding it delightful to hear this man speak out with his own individualistic approach.

The questions continued. But there are only so many questions to ask, so many comments to make, and then it appears the conversation is warmed over and stale. The committee had reviewed for the second time just about all the areas of concern or interest covered previously and were about to end the interview when Bender dropped a comment that straightened everyone up.

"Let's talk a minute about the parsonage."

All eyes looked at him.

"I am sure it was apparent to Dick and Marion, who were kind enough to show us around, that both Isabelle and I were extremely disappointed in the parsonage. It seems rather inadequate to raise a family, particularly when compared to the very fine home we now have in Ohio."

"Well, you recognize, Mr. Bender," exclaimed Dar, "that the parsonage is to be redecorated. In fact, the kitchen will be completely remodeled. We are just waiting until we can find a minister in order to allow him and his wife the opportunity to have the decorating and remodeling done to suit their taste."

"It isn't just that," said Bender. "The whole place is inadequate."

"That bathroom!" Isabella almost whispered. "It's really not very complete."

Dick Walker laughed ruefully. "It must have been built in the early twenties. The tub stands on legs, but I hear that style is coming back."

There was a heavy silence in the room. Each knew how justified the prospective minister's comments were. Yet, the parsonage had become through the years a symbol of something meaningful to the church. Some of the members had been married in its parlor and many had been counseled there. For the congregation as a whole, this house held many pleasant memories.

Bender cleared his throat and broke the silence. "Have you ever considered the possibility of selling the parsonage and building something a little more suitable? It is in a good location, and for an older couple with no family, it would be ideal. The money derived from its sale would go a long way toward supplying a home more adequate for the needs of your minister and his family."

Aird had to agree with him and did so. "The unfortunate thing, however," he said, "is that the place has an esteem in the minds of the congregation that is not justified by reality. I am sure that at the present time our congregation has no thought at all of doing such a thing as you suggest. I would like to suggest that if a call is made to you by the pulpit committee, you can consider the parsonage question as remaining open. Then, if you decide to accept the call to our church, we would face the parsonage question squarely with the congregation and attempt to obtain the approval of the church members to do as you suggest."

Bender sank back into his chair. This seemed to satisfy him. After a few more perfunctory remarks, the Benders took their leave of the group, and Gil Frazer drove them back to their motel. It was agreed that the committee would make a decision quickly as to whether or not to call him to the church, and, in turn, he assured them that their letter would get his prompt consideration and reply.

It took the committee all of fifteen minutes to make a decision after he left, and most of that time was spent on the substance and form of the letter to be sent to him. All agreed that Bender was the man. The letter would be mailed the next morning. It looked as though the search was over.

thirteen

THE PULPIT COMMITTEE had attempted to keep the visit of the Benders to Cedar City completely under cover. They soon found out that their efforts were unsuccessful and that Carl and Isabelle Bender had been seen with various members of the pulpit committee in town and at the church. While no one in the church outside of the pulpit committee members themselves knew who the Benders were, it did not take much deduction to arrive at the conclusion that these strange faces belonged to a prospective candidate and his wife, and the fact that they were visiting the church was a strong indication that the pulpit committee was nearing a point of decision.

So the wait for Bender's answer to the committee's call was a matter of anticipation not only to the five committee members but to a good share of the church membership as well. After some days went by and no answer had been received, the anticipation changed to impatience. Originally everyone thought that, allowing four days for the mail to travel in both directions and five days for the Benders to arrive at a decision, the whole matter would be settled in nine days at the most. A pulpit committee meeting had been scheduled accordingly to make final arrangements for the announcement to the church membership and to get the necessary church membership concurrence.

The pulpit committee meeting was held on schedule, but it was held without the receipt of an answer, either aye or nay, from Mr. Bender.

With no other business to attend to, the committee decided to make a determination of how best to handle his introduction to the congregation. According to the constitution of the church, an affirmative vote by at least two-thirds of the members present at an official business meeting was necessary to call officially a man to the pulpit. Such an official business meeting had to be announced by the moderator at the Sunday services for three weeks prior to the date of the meeting. The committee wasn't satisfied, however, to receive the support of only two-thirds of the congregation on such a vital vote. They considered what would have to be done to secure the support of all the congregation for their candidate.

To a great many in the church, just the fact that the man was recommended by their pulpit committee would be enough. But there were also a number of independents who would want to see for themselves and make their own choice. In his first written report to the congregation shortly after the pulpit committee was formed, Aird had advised them that when a candidate was found, he would be asked to speak to the church from the pulpit so that the congregation might appraise him prior to making their decision. At that time, Alice Larcher had taken exception to this approach stating that it seemed a rather cruel and callous situation in which to place a candidate. She felt, with some justification, Aird thought, that to put a man up in front of several hundred people to preach a trial sermon would be embarrassing not only to him but to those who had to listen and appraise him. Also, she felt that it would be extremely awkward for the candidate in his home church if the congregation, after listening to him, should turn down the pulpit committee's recommendation. After listening to her explanation, Aird and the rest of the committee concurred. However, the report had been sent out, and there was nothing to do but ignore the issue until the committee was faced with the problem. It looked now as though that time had come.

Alice asked the question. "How do we intend to introduce Reverend Bender and his wife to the church?"

Aird had discussed this with Bender when they had met together on the Saturday morning, and he repeated to Alice and the committee what the candidate had said. "Well, Bender feels that he would prefer not to preach a trial sermon. He did say, though, that he would be willing to visit us on a weeknight, possibly timed to coincide with the midweek meeting, and talk to the congregation and also answer any questions they might have. If we agreed, he would bring his family with him so that the congregation could meet them all."

Alice smiled and nodded her approval. "I think that would work out fine," she said. "We could have a family potluck supper."

"Sure," said Dick, "he would give the devotions, and then there could be a question-and-answer period that would allow everyone to really get to know him."

"That's what he would do best." It was Dar this time. "I think he would make a more favorable impression in an informal setting like that than if he preached a sermon."

"Dar doesn't think much of his preaching," teased Marion. Dar laughed.

"Oh, I guess he's all right. It's just that I was more impressed with him when he just chewed the fat."

Aird asked Alice if she would make the necessary arrangements for Bender's appearance at a midweek family night. She agreed to do so. That ended the business for the night. There was nothing to do now but wait for his letter. Aird assured everyone that he would promptly call each of them as soon as it arrived and that a meeting would be held immediately after to complete the plans. They adjourned to wait. There seemed to be nothing else they could do.

Two more days went by — still no letter. On Thursday, March 2, Aird called the others only to tell them he had received nothing. The consensus of thinking was that this was a good sign. If he were to say no, he would have done so promptly. Friday morning Aird felt surely this would be the day. He told Dorothy before leaving home in the morning to call him at his office if a letter arrived, but when by noon he had not heard from her, he resigned himself to another day's disappointment. There was still Saturday's mail to come, and this would still be time enough for Hal Larcher to make the first of the three required readings of the church membership meeting notice on Sunday morning. Then at two-thirty the call came through. Aird's secretary, knowing how anxiously he was awaiting the news, called him from a meeting to take the message. He picked up the receiver and heard Dorothy say that the letter had arrived.

"Good, now we can start moving on. . . ."

"Jack, — he's not coming!"

He was stunned! Then said, "Read the letter."

Dorothy did so. It was very nicely written — smooth, cordial. He wasn't coming. A pulpit committee meeting was called for that same evening.

The five sat and looked at each other in gloomy silence. Marion had brought out all the old resumés: those they had previously rejected and those with whom she had had correspondence and then tucked away for a rainy day. Well, the rainy day was here, and there was not a likely candidate among the bunch, or so it seemed.

Finally Marion spoke.

"Maybe it's about time," she said, "that we discard the guidelines we have set up. Let's lift the age barriers and any other barriers that we've set up and look only for the man instead of a list of statistics!"

Such a comment spoken a couple of months back would have received plenty of rebuttal. Now the only response it prompted was support.

"You know, I think Marion is right," Dar said. "What we want is a man who can do the things that our church needs, and it doesn't matter what age he is."

Aird listened with interest. There was a new attitude developing here, and at the moment he wasn't sure just what it was. But it did come close to answering a concern that had been bothering him about the matter of searching out a minister. He determined to talk to Robert Worden about it at the first opportunity.

"There is another matter that should concern us at this time." Alice was speaking. She had everyone's attention. "We have been on this task now for a long time. At first the church expected us to have a minister for Christmas. Then, they were sure that we would have one for Easter. At this very moment they all know that we have been in close contact with someone. I think they are quite sure that we have made an offer. While they don't know it is Bender, there is no doubt in my mind that the majority of the congregation expects us to announce in the next week or two that we have found a minister. The letdown when nothing happens will be pretty hard. We are but three weeks from Easter Sunday. It is not an easy time without a minister, even when we have someone filling in as well as Bob Waite has done for us."

"What would you suggest, Alice?" Aird asked.

"It would seem to me that it's necessary for us to make an oral report to the church this coming Sunday and let them know just where we stand. It's better that they receive the bad news direct from us than to have it filter down to them a little bit at a time."

"We can prepare a statement and have the moderator read it Sunday morning."

"I don't think that's sufficient," Alice went on. "I think that this is something that you, as chairman of the pulpit committee, ought to do." Aird looked around the room, hoping against hope that someone would have an alternative suggestion. No luck. Everyone was in agreement.

Sunday was only three days away. Determining what to say and how to say it so that the church could recognize the disappointment the committee had received, without becoming totally discouraged, would take up most of Aird's time and thoughts for the next two days.

Meanwhile, Marion once again would make contact with her various sources for the solicitation of new names to consider.

Aird and his wife Dorothy found seats down near the front at the end of a pew so that the walk to the pulpit would be as short as possible. When Hal Larcher announced to the congregation that the chairman of the pulpit committee had requested time to make a report, Aird found that even the few feet from the third-row pew to the pulpit seemed like an endless journey. He walked slowly up the aisle. The choir sat at the back of the chancel and watched solemnly as he approached. Dar was seated in the chancel directly behind the pulpit, having led the congregation in a responsive reading, filling his capacity as chairman of the board of deacons. He looked solid. The smile, the honest, straightforward gaze as Aird took his place was one of full support, full understanding, and Aird felt better just knowing that he was there. Aird turned around to face the congregation and reached into his pocket and pulled out a sheaf of notes. The noise of the paper rustled over the loudspeaker system like a faint rumble of thunder. Aird swallowed a couple of times and looked over the congregation. For the first time, he realized that the sanctuary was filled. It seemed to him that there was an unearthly silence to the place. One could expect some rustle, some coughing, some evidence of life, but nothing of the sort seemed to be evident here. Even the faces that looked up appeared vacant, expressionless. He started to speak.

"I wish to thank Reverend Waite for so graciously allowing me to use the time allotted to his sermon this morning to bring to you a report from your pulpit committee.

"We have postponed doing this for several weeks because it appeared likely that we would be able to recommend to you shortly a candidate for our pulpit. This has not turned out to be the case, and we do not have a candidate at the present time to recommend to you.

"We have just completed six months of intensified effort in this task that you have assigned to Alice Larcher, Marion Frazer, Dick Walker, Darwin Wood, and me. During this time twenty-six committee meetings have been held. We have studied close to one hundred resumés of ministers submitted to us by all the major denominational seminaries and from the various local, state, and national offices. These resumés have been studied and sifted to remove those who obviously did not meet the qualifications of our church. Those that remained, and they numbered about fifty, were contacted by letter. These contacts have resulted in thirteen visits by members of our committee to six midwest and eastern states. These visits have produced no more than two candidates whom we considered capable of adequately filling the needs of our church.

"Just what are these standards that so restrict our efforts to find the right man?"

As he spoke, Aird looked out over the congregation. He tried to locate the other members of the committee. Alice usually sat in the right section near the front. Marion and Dick both would be seated in the left section toward the rear. But he could see none of them. Actually, he was having trouble making out the faces of anyone in the congregation. This bothered him. He would have liked to observe the facial reactions to what he was saying. He continued:

"We are a unique church. As one of the oldest and most centrally located in Cedar City, our influence and ministry extend far beyond the walls of our building. Our minister must have the capacity to understand, to feel, to respond to the needs of our community. He must be capable of supplying pastoral guidance to the unchurched citizens on the street. At the other end of the spectrum he is expected to be a moral and spiritual influence on the civic, business, and community leaders of our town.

"But even more than all this, the man we are looking for must in a very unique way fill the spiritual needs of our church family; for in spite of our downtown location this is essentially a family church. We delight in our children and want the type of ministry that will stimulate live, dynamic, well-grounded programs for them. We are concerned that so many of our young people drift away from the church family when they reach the age of young adulthood. These young people require a challenging ministry. They insist on intellectual honesty. Any hint of hypocrisy or sham in the presentation of the Christian message automatically turns them off. The minister we find must be able to accept and respond to their challenging questions and their honest doubts.

"Our church is grateful and proud of our senior citizens. Their faithfulness and loyalty has been the strength of the church for many years. In thinking of the needs of the young, we must not neglect them. The maturity, warmth, and friendliness expected of a minister by our senior citizens are qualities that would be helpful to all of us.

"And what about the rest of us, the group between the young and the old, often looked on as the working force? What do we need? This is a question that has given your committee much thought and prompted considerable discussion.

"In these troubled days when many are uncertain whether God is alive or dead we need a man who will present the Christian message loud and clear. We are not looking for a campaigner who would remake the world and more particularly our church into whatever shape his perhaps misguided zeal directed. But neither do we want a man who is so afraid of the world around him that he would wrap us in a cocoon of cliché-type thoughts and outmoded traditions that insult our intelligence and Christian faith. To borrow a phrase from Reverend Waite's fine sermon of last week, 'We just don't want to be fenced in.'

"We want real Christian leadership, free of preachments or vague abstract theories. In short, we want someone to feed our spiritual hunger and to direct our energetic but often misspent efforts so that our church will continue to grow, prosper, and fill a vital need in our community and family lives.

"This, then, is the man we search for. Is it any wonder that we have found so few who measure up to these standards?"

When he mentioned Bob Waite's name, Aird half-turned to face the interim minister who was seated to the right of the pulpit. Then having turned that far around, Aird kept turning until he faced the choir sitting behind him. They were all awake – not only awake, but listening. With his back to the microphone, however, his voice had faded out, and he turned quickly back to face the front.

"You might ask, 'But what of the two or three who did appear to meet our qualifications?' We must confess to disappointments. In at least two cases, men who we thought might be ideally suited for our church accepted other pastorates before we had a chance to visit them. A third prime candidate decided, after much thought and consideration, to remain with his present church. One of the biggest difficulties in finding the right man is that such a man is usually very successful, well liked, and happy in his present situation. Such a man is hard to move.

"Also, you ought to know that in some ways what we are prepared to offer financially is much less than a suitable candidate has a right to expect and is in most cases now receiving.

"For example, the parsonage we supply is far inferior to that now lived in by most of the ministers we have visited. The salary shown in our annual budget is lower than the salary received by any candidate that we have seriously considered. Fortunately, our board of trustees recognizes these problems and has allowed the committee some leeway in these matters.

"There are those who will think that our standards are too high, that we should settle for something less. Perhaps we may have to settle for something less. It depends really on how much patience you have — how long you are willing to continue as you are.

"When I was very young, a tenet of my faith was God's promise that he would never fail us or forsake us. In the years that have since gone by, I have had reason to revise or even discard many of my beliefs and religious ideas, but this one has remained unchanged — mainly because it is a promise that to date has never been broken. In every adversity, a way has always opened.

"I believe the emergence of unusually fine lay leadership in our church during the present trying times only reinforces my belief in that promise. The work that our lay people have done in maintaining the business and spiritual life of the church has been superb. The presence of Mr. Waite in our pulpit during this time has filled a great void. He has sustained our church when the need was the greatest, and the work of our pulpit committee is made that much easier because he is here.

"During the next several months, the committee will once again be traveling, meeting, and appraising new candidates. We believe that somewhere in our Baptist fellowship is the right man for our church. We want you to know that we are trying awfully hard. Backed by your prayers and God's help, we will find him."

Aird picked up his unused notes and jammed them back into his coat pocket. Public speaking wasn't new to him, but usually such an event could be measured by audience response — either by applause, laughter, or facial expression. He had heard no sound for the entire fifteen minutes he had spent talking. Neither had there been evidenced any expression at all, favorable or unfavorable, that he could discern. He walked slowly back to his seat and sat down, vowing that this would be the first and last time that he would stand before these people empty-handed. If the committee still held the membership's confidence, they would go after this thing with an effort exceeding anything exhibited to date.

fourteen

The appointment with Dr. Worden was for 1:30 p.m. The southwest section of town was in the throes of repair and reconstruction, and the block in which Worden's office was located was an island in the sea of rubble. When Aird had finally made his way through the maze of detours that blocked his way, he was five minutes late. Fortunately, so was Worden. They met in the driveway and walked into the office building together. Aird hadn't seen Dr. Worden since the first meeting of the committee the previous September. Since then, Worden had traveled around the world visiting denominational mission centers and undoubtedly had been involved in countless other projects besides. The purpose of this visit was once again to solicit his help in the search.

Worden's office displayed mementoes picked up in the Far East during his trip, as well as some that he had acquired on previous journeys. Aird studied these with interest. When they finally got down to discussing the reason for the visit, Worden showed that he had not lost his interest or concern in the Cedar City church. He had followed closely the committee's efforts and was well aware of the events that had taken place to date. He recounted all the candidates for whom he had supplied dossiers and expressed once again his thoughts on those who he felt were most acceptable. Aird drummed his fingers on the arm of his chair and finally broke in impatiently. "Dr. Worden, there must be someone better than these."

Worden looked up from the sheaf of papers, a startled look on his face. "I'm sorry," Aird said. "I know this sounds rather rude, but we have already reviewed these men and others just like them several times over. They're not for us. We need someone different."

"Are you sure you know what you want?"

It was not said unkindly. Nevertheless, Aird paused for a moment before answering.

"No. No, I guess we aren't. But we believe that we will know him when we find him." They sat quietly, neither speaking. Aird looked over Dr. Worden's head at a mahogany carving that had come from the Philippines. Worden looked down at the papers on his desk. When Worden finally spoke, it was slowly and deliberately.

"There's a chap down in Indiana, Jack. I've had my eye on him for a long time. He's a good man, a very good man. His doctorate is earned. He presents a good appearance and has deep convictions. He is originally out of the Southern Baptist Convention, but I would say, theologically speaking, the American Baptist Convention is where he belongs. I don't know if you can entice him to Cedar City or not. But if you can, there's no doubt in my mind that you would have a top-notch man."

"He's a conservative?"

Dr. Worden looked at Aird quizzically. "Yes, I suppose you could say he's of the conservative school."

"Bob, have you noted that every candidate you have recommended to us has been conservative?"

A slight smile crossed his face. "No, I hadn't noted. Though, this could very well be true. There are a lot of very fine men with what you might call a conservative theology who deserve to be supported and encouraged."

"That's the problem," Aird tried to keep the tone of his voice even, but he could feel bitterness creeping into every word he spoke. "Until we started looking for a minister, most of our committee didn't know a liberal from a conservative and couldn't have cared less. But obviously it's a big thing to the people to whom we go for help. We're looking for a man with ability, with motivation, with the special peculiar spark that ignites the lives of the people to whom he ministers. It seems to me there are too few of them around to have to further classify them as to their theological leanings."

He had expected this outburst to result in a protestation from Dr. Worden. It didn't come. Instead, he brushed the papers aside and leaned forward across the desk. "Believe me, Jack, my office has not withheld any name from consideration. Not only that, we will search out any name that you give us. If we have seemed to push some candidates towards your consideration more than others, it is because we are tempted to feel that our knowledge of your church and the people available make us uniquely qualified to offer recommendations. But we want you to know that our complete files are at your disposal at any time." Aird sat back in his chair.

The air had been cleared. Perhaps he had been unfair, but if so, at least he felt assured in his own mind that Dr. Worden understood and appreciated the concern of the pulpit committee on this matter.

The return drive to Cedar City seemed considerably shorter than the drive over.

fifteen

It was one of those bright, clear, spring days with just a nip of chill in the air and the bright sky was laced with wisps of powdery white clouds. The foliage along the toll road was lush and green, and patterns were already taking shape in the rich, black soil on either side of the expressway as farmers prepared for sowing.

It was great to be alive, and the car was filled with bright, inconsequential chatter. The group had left Cedar City heading west just prior to lunchtime and, although on the road but thirty minutes, Dorothy and Marion were already looking for a likely spot to stop and spread out the picnic lunch they had prepared for the occasion. There were several fine roadside parks along the highway, but as yet the picnic tables had not been brought back from their winter storage. Finally, Gil spotted a picnic area along the Grand River, just north of the highway. Aird wheeled the car off at the next exit and worked back to the spot.

When the two couples got out of the car, they found that the ground was muddy. The shade provided by the trees, which looked so inviting when viewed from the pavement, now was but a shield keeping out the warmth of the sun. But no one really cared. Their spirits were high, and they laughed as they threaded their way between the puddles and mud to a picnic table situated on high, dry ground. There the women spread out the picnic lunch and poured the hot coffee. The river was moving rapidly, and around a small bend on an old wooden bridge three youngsters were trying their luck with bamboo fishing poles. The food was good. The coffee was hot. The setting was picturesque, and they had the optimism that spurred each trip taken in search of a minister. It was a bright, happy moment.

Certainly their attitude wasn't based on any results to date, nor on any particular promise held for the trip they were now on. During the month since Aird had met with Dr. Worden the committee had visited several candidates. None of them seemed to fit the job. Now once again new visits were being made. Dick Walker and Dar Wood were on their way to the southern part of Illinois to visit one of the "over fifty but strong in experience and ability" group. Alice Larcher and her husband, Hal, were combining a vacation trip to Iowa with a visit to a minister from that state who appeared to have first-rate credentials. The Airds and Frazers were to visit a candidate in the Chicago area, stopping on the way to meet Rev. W. D. Booth, whose name had also come up for consideration. All in all, there was no particular reason to be optimistic. The candidate being visited by Dick and Dar had been previously rejected as over-age. Mr. Booth was also in the fifty-year category.

John Lovell, the man in the Chicago area, had been the minister of only one church and was now serving as an associate pastor. Such qualifications hardly seemed adequate for the position to be filled.

Nevertheless, the travelers showed no sign of weariness in spite of the strong possibility that once again the trip might be unproductive. Back on the road they sped toward the Indiana Turnpike, across the northwest tip of Indiana, and then toward Chicago fighting the late Saturday afternoon traffic. The area was not pleasant. They checked the car windows to make sure the stench of billowing smoke, gasoline fumes, and other industrial contamination was closed out as much as possible. The drab grayness of old factory buildings mingled with the equally drab grayness of old residential homes. The hustle and bustle of factory activity, which normally would offer some excuse for the dreary landscape, was gone on this Saturday afternoon, and there was a feeling of death hanging over the industrial complexes. The cramped residential streets pushed in between the factories along the way seemed stunted and sickly. Even the children on the streets appeared to be tired and bored.

It was in this location that they found Mr. Booth. An hour and a half later it was a subdued group that headed north.

The prospective minister, Rev. W. D. Booth, had not looked like a man of the cloth. His hair was steel gray and cropped close in what was the next thing to a crew cut. The face was roughhewn, irregular, and strong. His eyes had the quick, alert look of an active man, his mind uncluttered with doubts or fears.

His hands were those of a construction worker, which as it turned out, he was by avocation, having spent his last two vacations constructing mission buildings.

Mrs. Booth was a big woman with an expansive radiant smile. The living room where she seated the four pulpit committee visitors reflected the homeliness of both herself and her husband. The room was clean but well used. The numerous chairs were large and well cushioned, making up in comfort for what was lacking in style. On the fireplace mantle was a row of six portraits – their six children. On the wall behind the sofa there hung a plaque proclaiming that "Christ is the unseen guest in this house."

Mrs. Booth explained about the children. The three youngest were at home. One boy was attending the local junior college, the oldest was away at college. "And Billy on the end there," said Mrs. Booth, "the one in uniform, he's in Vietnam." Her voice softened ever so slightly as she said this last. No trace of bitterness, or pride, or sadness – her voice, if it indicated anything, reflected resignation.

Aird felt a pang of anguish as he listened to her words and looked at the boyish, earnest face on the portrait. Here was the strength of America – this family – this boy – strong, virile, clean, who had so much to offer and would unquestioningly give it all when called. God help America! God help its leaders if they sacrificed these lives unwisely.

Marion was asking Mr. Booth about his church. When he answered, it seemed as though his face clouded over.

"If you went through town, you passed it on the way here."

She informed him that she had seen the building.

"Then you know that it's old, and big, and ugly. Also, it's usually pretty empty."

"Empty?"

"This is a predominately Catholic town," he explained. "You can't realize how hard it is to attract new members. Our only hope is to attract newcomers coming in to take jobs in the factories, but even there, we find there is not much opportunity for us."

Gil Frazer asked him why he didn't build a smaller church in the suburbs.

"We've thought of that, but there don't seem to be any buyers for our present building. Unless we can raise money in this way, we haven't got the finances for a new church. You see, with our small congregation, it takes all the money we have to pay the upkeep on our present facility." He paused for a minute and then added, "I guess you might say that we can't afford to stay and we can't afford to leave. It's sort of a trapped feeling. Perhaps a new man, a younger man, with new ideas, a fresh approach, might find the answer."

Other questions were asked, and he, in turn, asked questions about the Cedar City church. But both he and the committee knew at parting time that they would not meet again.

The road now was north. Neither the Frazers nor the Airds had been to Holly, where the Lovells lived. John Lovell had advised that they stop at one of the motels in the area of O'Hare Airport and call from there. It was a two-hour drive on toll-road highways to the airport. They would arrive shortly after seven, which wouldn't leave much time for dinner before visiting the Lovells. They settled back to relax. Marion pulled out the resumé of Lovell and read it aloud while there was still some sunlight. Thirty-five years of age — born in Brooklyn, New York — educated at New York

City College and Columbia University – graduated from Colgate Rochester Divinity School – total previous experience, college chaplain and minister in upstate New York. He was a New Yorker through and through. Aird wondered how he would fit with the midwest conservatism of Cedar City. He reread again in his mind Lovell's reply to the first overture to him. It was smooth, candid, confident, and a trifle aggressive. It had a touch of youth and bravado. But would it be palatable to the Cedar City people? While Aird was mulling over this, Marion was giving further particulars of his present ministry. "He has been six years at Holly as co-pastor of the Grace Baptist Church. That's a long time to be a co-pastor."

"It's also an awfully high salary they're paying him for such a limited responsibility," Aird added.

"Well, I think perhaps the title is misleading," said Marion. "It appears that he shares all the duties of the ministry with the senior minister, who is considerably older than Mr. Lovell."

"I don't think you should give any thought to salaries right now," Dorothy put in. "Your job now is to find the right man. The salary is secondary. There will be time enough to think about that when you find the man you want."

Gil wanted to know about Lovell's wife. "Well, let's see." Marion scanned through the resumé. "Her name is Alice. That should be easy – think of Alice Larcher. Her educational background is good. She was graduated from Hunter College and received her master's degree. She's a native New Yorker, too. Two small children, a boy and a girl, and she's a music teacher."

It was getting dark. Marion put the resumé back in

the folder. They drove on in silence as day turned to night. The highway was filling up with traffic. In the distance could be seen the lights of O'Hare Airport Drive. The timing had been accurate. At seven-thirty, they were checking into the motel. Twenty minutes later, they were in the coffee shop eating a quick snack while waiting for Mr. Lovell to arrive.

After they had finished eating, Aird visited the motel desk to inquire about messages while the others waited in the lobby. When he returned, Lovell was there. Aird observed him closely. Medium in height, he had a strong build with the sloping shoulders of an athlete. He turned as Aird walked up. "And you're Jack Aird! I'm Pastor John! After our several phone conversations, I feel like I already know you." They discovered later that "instant friendship" came easily to him. "My car's out front. Alice is in it waiting for us."

"We can follow you in our car if you like. It would save you a trip back later this evening."

"Not at all – not at all. No need for that. Alice and I enjoy getting out for a drive. Besides, it will give us that much more time with you – that is, if you don't mind all crowding together in one car." He laughed as he spoke. The women assured him that they didn't mind crowding a little. Actually there was no need for concern. His car turned out to be a large four-year-old blue Cadillac, and they all fitted in comfortably. "'It belongs to Alice," he explained a little sheepishly. "I usually drive a little runabout."

Gil, Marion, and Dorothy climbed into the back seat. Aird joined Alice in the front. Even seated, it was evident that she was short in stature. Her complexion and hair were dark like her husband's and, like his, her eyes were bright and lively. She continued Pastor John's explanation about the car as he slid in behind the wheel. "We bought it for a trip we took last year to the west coast. John was spending a month at a seminar at U.C.L.A., and the whole family went with him, in cluding my mother and his. It was a real riot!" She broke out in a hearty laugh, and her mouth opened wide showing two rows of gleaming white teeth.

"I talked informally to some of the trustees when I bought it," continued Pastor John, "and told them that if they thought it was too pretentious for their minister, I would sell it when we returned from our trip. So far there has been nothing said about it. Anyway, I hardly drive it — except on special occasions like this." The infectious laugh started again, but it was drowned out by his wife's roar of appreciation at his wittiness.

Aird looked at her with renewed interest. She was a personality! After almost a year of exposure to nervous, fluttery, cautious, or timid ministers' wives, here he was confronted with a real live personality who would have to be noticed and measured in her own right. She might never make it as a bishop's wife, but this gave promise of being a stimulating and exciting evening — besides, the Baptist church didn't have bishops.

Ten minutes away from the motel, they were clear of the commercial district and driving through a pleasant suburban area. "This is our town," John told them. "Our home is just a few minutes away." The Lovells' residence was an attractive colonial home situated behind the church and facing a municipal park.

When they were seated inside, the group met the Lovells' children, Philip and Sharon, who had stayed up past their bedtime for this particular ceremony. Also, they met Alice's mother. She was a charming Armenian lady with all the grace and courtesy of the old world. When the pulpit committee finally got around to talking shop with Pastor John, the awkwardness of self-consciousness that so often had been present at such occasions was conspicuously absent.

During the course of the evening the committee covered all the standard questions that many months of interviewing had made a fixed part of their approach, and yet it didn't seem like an interview at all. Rather, in general conversation most of the things they would have asked just seemed to come out. In the discussions, Alice took as lively and spirited a part as John. In fact, later, it was not too clear in Aird's mind just what point of view represented her thinking and which was his. Reflecting about this, he felt that their thinking was compatible on all questions, with hers perhaps being more tolerant than his.

It wasn't until the evening was over and they were being driven back to the motel that Aird realized that neither John Lovell nor Alice had asked questions about Cedar City or the church. Any apparent interest that they had shown had been directed to the committee personally. The good-nights at the door were loud and spirited. When they drove away, the four looked at each other and each drew a deep, slow, relaxing breath. "Well?" Aird asked. Gil and Dorothy both started to speak at once and then stopped and laughed.

"O.K. You say it!" said Gil.

"There's no doubt," exclaimed Dorothy, "he's the one! We just have to get this man." Aird looked at Gil. He was smiling like a man who had struck oil.

"That's my sentiment, too. We've found our man.

We don't have to look any further." Aird looked at Marion.

"I wonder how he will do in the pulpit?"

"Oh, I hope he does well," she answered. "I really hope he does well."

The church that John Lovell served had two morning services, one at nine-thirty and one at the hour of eleven. The two ministers preached on alternate Sundays with the one not preaching taking the remaining functions of the service. The Airds and Frazers attended the nine-thirty service. Pastor Steve, the senior minister, led the worship service. He was a man in his late fifties — perhaps older — the type of person whose age was not easily determined. He had a trim build, a soft, modulated voice. His whole appearance was that of a man at peace with the world. It was easy to see how he could share the pulpit and work of the church with a young, dynamic, ambitious man. This man had no fear of competition. This was his church. These were his people. He was completely at home. If first appearances made for a fair observation, here was a true love affair between minister and congregation. As the service unfolded, and Pastor John assisted the older man in the simple ceremony of the acceptance of new members, it was apparent that a bond of respect and affection held these two also. It made the visitors wonder if anyone had the right to attempt to break up what appeared to be such a harmonious and successful relationship.

Then Pastor John preached. Measured academically, it was a good sermon. Perhaps not as good as some that they had heard on their many visitations, but better than most. But aside from the structure of the sermon, there was something else. There appeared to be a personal involvement of the man with his preaching. When he spoke of wrong and sin, his voice had the sound of indignation. When he spoke of the defeats of people, his face had a true look of sorrow, and when he spoke of hope and promise of victories, his voice rang and his eyes were bright. When he had concluded, the listener didn't try to analyze or dissect what had been said. He just felt that somehow he had been part of an experience and felt much the better for that experience.

The four returned to Cedar City believing that they had finally found their man.

sixteen

DICK AND DAR HAD PICKED A LOSER. They returned to Cedar City discouraged once again. Later, however, when they heard about Lovell, their old optimism returned. They were eager to meet him first hand. Since Alice Larcher would be out of town one more week, the committee decided that the two men would make the trip right away.

By the time Alice returned, all four of the others had been won over to Alice and John Lovell. As they listened to her report of her visit to Iowa at the pulpit committee meeting on the Monday night following her return, it was difficult to control the urge to interrupt and tell her that the search was over. The man had finally been found.

However, as Alice continued to speak, there was an awareness that she, too, had found someone who just might do the job. Where just a week ago there had been no qualified candidate, now it appeared there might be two! Alice concluded her report by saying, "I don't think that Mr. Root is outstanding in every respect, but I feel that he is a very capable man who can contribute a great deal to our church and who is worthy of further consideration." This was high tribute indeed from Alice, who was not inclined to gild the lily at any time.

"Alice, while you were away, the rest of us visited this man Lovell in Illinois, and we think we have found someone of particular interest." Aird spoke in measured tones. He wanted to be as objective about this as possible. He asked Marion to give a rundown on the first visit. When she had done so, Dar did the same on the visit that he and Dick had made. Alice listened quietly through it all. She not only heard what was said, but sensed also the excitement and feeling behind the words.

"It looks," she said after Dar had finished, "as though you feel that you have found the right man."

"That's right," he answered. "This fellow sure looks like he has what we've been looking for."

"But we want you to visit him and appraise him for yourself," Aird added. "Meanwhile," he went on a little lamely, "some others should visit Mr. Root. Your evaluation of him indicates that we should make further contact with him."

Alice was not to be fooled by this attempt at objectivity.

"No," she said, "while I think Mr. Root is a good man, he doesn't project in me, nor will he in you, the kind of enthusiasm that all of you show toward Mr. Lovell. If Mr. Root were located nearby, it would be nice for someone to visit him, but to make that long trip to Iowa? I just don't think that under the circumstances it would be justified. No, I believe we had better dispose of the Lovell question before we give any further consideration to Mr. Root. That seems to be the wiser course."

There was almost a sigh of relief around the room. Alice had sized up the situation perfectly and voiced the approach that seemed most reasonable to all.

"When do you think you can visit Mr. Lovell?" Marion asked.

"Oh, I don't think it is necessary for me to make a visit," Alice answered. "If the four of you feel that he is the candidate you want, I think our next step is to invite him to Cedar City. I will have an opportunity to talk to him and appraise him at that time. If he is the right man, we must try to conclude this matter as quickly as possible."

Dick grinned broadly. "I thought that might be the thinking, so when Dar and I visited Pastor John, we asked him for a suitable date for a visit."

"And what was the date?"

"May 5th — it falls on a Friday."

Once the invitation to visit Cedar City had been made, and the first flush of enthusiasm had waned, the committee began to look at John Lovell in a more realistic light. Just what did they know about him? The references included in his resumés could hardly be considered unbiased. His work history showed that his past experience was limited to two churches, and in only one of these had he been senior minister. He had been recommended by Colgate Rochester, but then, so had several others before him that the committee had thought to be wanting. And certainly his name took a long time in coming to the surface. What was needed were first-hand references. Alice Larcher arranged to speak to Dr. Roger Turnbull, the head of Religious Affairs for the state university. He had been a member of the Cedar City church at one time. Alice Larcher had known him when he was just a little boy. She was confident that he could be depended upon to give a fair and invaluable appraisal of John Lovell. Because they were both about the same age and both had attended Colgate Rochester Divinity School, it was likely that they were acquainted.

In reviewing in his mind the initial interview with Lovell, Aird recalled that he had mentioned that a former classmate was now the minister of the First Baptist Church in Blissfield. His name was Earl Patton, and just one year ago he had succeeded Dr. James, who had retired after many years in the Blissfield church. The backgrounds of Patton and Lovell were similar in many respects. Both had gone to Colgate Rochester at about the same time. Also, if Lovell came to Cedar City, he would be facing a situation not too dissimilar from Blissfield. The churches in size, character of membership, and outlook were very much alike. A visit to the Blissfield church's worship service, he concluded, might very well give a hint as to the type of service John Lovell might conduct. Also, Patton's success — or lack of it — in Blissfield would be an indicator of sorts as to the probability of John Lovell being successful in Cedar City. Aird decided to visit Blissfield.

Sunday morning started off badly right from the beginning. Blissfield was an hour and fifteen minutes, drive from Cedar City. Allowing fifteen minutes for picking up Airds' daughter, Janis, at Blissfield College meant that a full hour and a half allowance must be made for the trip if they were to be on time for the church service. It had been a rush getting away from the house, and as Aird entered his garage, he felt instinctively for wallet, glasses, and car keys. He had them all, but when he opened the garage door in order to back the car out, he found the driveway blocked by his wife's car which had been used by their son on his Saturday night date. Did Dorothy have her car keys in her bag? No. The garage door leading into the house had locked behind them. Aird walked around the house to the front entrance. He had a key for that door on his key ring. But the storm door was latched! He rang the doorbell. He tried hollering, but he feared he might wake the neighbors. He pitched pebbles at his son's bedroom window until he was afraid the window would break. Then in desperation he climbed up the ladder of the T.V. aerial that was within reach of his son's bedroom window. Swaying there twenty-five feet off the ground in his blue serge suit, looking through the window at the blond, tousled head of his boy sleeping just out of reach, he said lovingly, but firmly, "If you don't get up and open that door, I'm going to kill you!"

They drove away in silence. Finally, Dorothy started to titter. "I wonder," she said, "what Alan's going to think when he finally wakes up enough to reason why you were outside trying to get in at nine o'clock on a Sunday morning."

"It won't enter his mind," Aird grunted, "that there was anything wrong." She started to laugh, and so did he. Then he looked at his watch. If the roads were clear and nothing further went wrong, they would reach the church just about the time the congregation was singing the opening hymn.

That is just how it worked out. Janis was waiting at the entrance to Lawrence Hall at Blissfield College, and Aird was fortunate enough to find a nearby parking place when they reached the church. They walked in the door of the sanctuary just as the congregation was rising to sing the opening hymn. But they weren't the only late arrivals, as there was a small traffic jam in the foyer leading into the sanctuary. Extra chairs were being put behind the last permanent row of pews to take care of the overflow. Probably the three of them could have slipped into this portable seating arrangement without too much fuss, but they trustfully put themselves in the hands of an usher who seemed to know what he was about. He led the way down the right center aisle, past the earlier arrivals at the rear, down past all of the church regulars who had staked out the middle pews, and even past those harried late souls who had been forced by their tardiness to the front of the sanctuary, until they reached the very front pew which had no occupants at all. There he left them, front and center, at the head of the entire congregation, eyeball to eyeball with the front row of sopranos standing in the choir.

The congregation was just swinging into the second verse of "The Church's One Foundation." Aird instinctively reached forward to pick up a hymnal from its proper place in the back of the pew in front of him. There was no pew and no hymnal. There was a slight nudge in his back between the shoulder blades, and he turned to see an open hymnal being offered. Aird tried to hide behind the hymnal and finished out the last three verses. It seemed as though those sopranos and he were singing at each other. After the last verse and a short prayer, when there was an opportunity to sit down, he glanced at the pulpit area in an attempt to pick out Mr. Patton. It wasn't easy to do. Sitting to the right of the choir was a robed minister, tall, dark, good-looking, about the age of thirty-five. Sitting to the left of the choir was a robed minister, tall, blond, good-looking, about the age of thirty-five. Which was Patton and which was the associate? When Mr. Patton did arise to give the sermon, they saw he was the blond.

While Aird sat there trying to determine who was who, he developed an uncomfortable suspicion that the ministers were also studying his little group. One looked amused, the other rather embarrassed, and Aird told himself that he was letting the rather conspicuous seating arrangement play tricks on his senses. He leaned over to express his thoughts to Janis, who was sitting between her mother and him, when he noticed her dress for the first time. It was short – perhaps not as miniskirts go, but a lot shorter than they should go in church. Sitting there on that church bench, it had managed to creep to new heights. He nudged her sharply. "Get that skirt down!" She wiggled a couple of times.

"That's it," she said. "That's as far as it goes." He looked down again and groaned softly. Sitting with a pew in front and a hymnal on her knees, some sort of decorum might have been maintained. As it was, there was nothing to do but look away. Aird looked straight ahead once more to the chancel. The sopranos in their ankle-length robes were looking down disapprovingly. The two young ministers were looking over the heads of the congregation toward the back of the church.

The service was a conventional Sunday morning worship service that was probably being repeated in dozens of churches throughout the country. But it had that little particular touch of force, enthusiasm, and sincerity that set it apart from many others that the Airds had attended. Mr. Patton's sermon showed evidence of considerable study and planning and was presented with confidence in an easy, smooth delivery. When the closing "Amen" had been said and the congregation started to file out of the pews, there was the feeling of having been a part of a good experience. If Lovell stood in the same tradition and could produce the same results, Aird was more anxious to have him as minister than ever.

At the church door Patton's associate was greeting the people, shaking their hands, and saying good-bye, with little time wasted in idle chatter. When the Airds reached him, a big smile broke across his face. "Well, hello. You are the folks who were sitting down front," he said. Dorothy agreed they were. "Try us again," he added.

"If we do," she answered, "we'll make sure to get here early."

Later that day, Aird called Patton. "We haven't met," he told him on the phone, "but I was at your service this morning with my wife and daughter, and, in fact, sat in the front pew." That was all he had to say. Patton remembered.

He also remembered the Lovells. "Sure, I know John and Alice well. I think John probably was a couple of years behind me in school, so our contact at that time wasn't too great. However, we have crossed paths several times since. Before coming to Blissfield, I was located not too many miles from where the Lovells are now. Every once in a while, we had the opportunity to get together with Alice and John. Frankly, I would be happy to see them come to your church if for no other reason than to have the opportunity to taste her cooking once again."

Aird laughed. This was the second time he had heard the same comment. When Alice Larcher had contacted Turnbull, he had spoken with enthusiasm about Alice Lovell's skill in the kitchen.

"But tell me," Aird asked, "do you feel that John Lovell would do the job in our church?"

There was no hesitancy at the other end of the line. "I would recommend him wholeheartedly!" Patton said. "John is a vigorous, dynamic, forward-thinking type of man. We don't have enough like him in our state convention, and he would be an asset not only to your church but to the Baptist work in this state."

Aird thanked Patton and laid down the phone. No further consideration was needed. He was ready for Lovell's visit.

seventeen

PLANS WERE SHAPING UP for Lovells' visit. The format would be similar to that used for the Benders, which had gone quite well. There would be one major difference, though. The committee would make their decision regarding John Lovell while he was still in Cedar City and would ask that he, in turn, either give an immediate answer or at least not delay his reply more than a day or two.

Up to now, the five committee members had discreetly refrained from discussing pulpit committee business with anyone. Now, however, they needed help. The discussions with John Lovell had clearly indicated that he would not accept the salary that the committee was authorized to offer. In order to resolve this problem George Davis, chairman of the board of trustees, and Walt Bosch, chairman of the trustees' finance committee, dropped over to see Aird the Wednesday night before the Lovells' visit.

On the first visit to see John Lovell, Aird had received a tape from him of the sermon preached that morning, with his Christmas sermon on the reverse side.

It had been a valuable aid to the committee. Dick and Dar had heard it prior to their visit, and it had been played for Alice Larcher at the meeting held following her return from Iowa. Aird decided to use it now.

Before playing the tape, he read to them excerpts from Lovell's resumé and told them some things about the interview. They had few questions and no adverse comments, as Aird had expected. He was more interested in their reactions to the tape. John Lovell's sermons, at least the two on the tape, were of the conventional type and depended on "heart" for appeal. Dr. Post had seemed to take particular pride in preaching sermons that were creations of art – sometimes poetic, sometimes dramatic, always intellectually stimulating. Certainly Walt Bosch was an enthusiastic fan of Dr. Post's preaching, and perhaps Davis was too. If there were to be criticisms of John Lovell's preaching style or content, they would come now. Aird started the tape and watched their faces closely. Except for an exclamation right at the beginning about the vigorous, clear quality of the voice, there was no reaction at all during the playing. Then when Aird walked over to turn it off, George Davis spoke up. "I thought you said there were two of them."

"You mean you want to hear the other sermon, too?" Aird looked over at Walt. He was studying the Lovell resumés, but he looked up now.

"Sure," he said. "Let's hear the other tape." Aird had his answer. Pastor John was home free.

When the tape had run out, they were ready to hear about the pulpit committee's problems.

Aird told them of the salary question. When he had finished speaking, Walt spoke immediately. "It seems to me that once we are satisfied that we have the right man, we should meet whatever price it takes to get him."

"It's going to take more than we have been authorized to offer, even with the increased range that the trustees recently voted for us."

"How much is it going to take?" George asked. Aird told him. "I'll canvass everyone on the board of trustees tomorrow," he said.

They talked further about the sale of the parsonage and the purchase of a new home. This called for a church membership meeting to vote on the trustee board's recommendation. The third reading of the announcement would be Sunday morning, and the meeting would be Sunday evening. Both George and Walt felt that the approval of the sale of the parsonage would be almost automatic. The purchase of a new parsonage would not be considered until the needs of the new minister were known. The housing problem promised to be resolved readily. As they broke up, George assured Aird that he would call the next evening with the result of his telephone canvass of the board.

He was true to his word. The next evening, just after supper, the phone rang. Aird got the results with the usual economy of words that Davis practiced on the phone. "O.K., Jack. You've got the go-ahead. The approval was 100 percent."

He was still basking in the gratification of this announcement when the phone rang again. It was one of the trustees. "Jack, I've been thinking of the call I received from George. That figure you gave as a maximum — does your committee really feel that this will do the job?" Aird told him he thought it would. "Well, another five hundred would round the figure out and if you find that kind of increase is necessary, I'll guarantee the additional amount for three years in addition to my regular pledge."

"But you don't know anything about this man!"

"I don't have to. If you people think he is the man for the church after the search you have made, that's good enough for me."

Aird put down the receiver in wonder. What a bunch! With this kind of backing, the committee just couldn't let these people down.

The Lovells arrived in Cedar City at 6 P.M. on a Friday. Shortly after checking into the motel, they were driven to the church, where Alice and Hal Larcher were waiting to act as their hosts on a tour of the church facilities. Alice and Hal were logical choices to perform such a function, since they knew the church and its history better than the others on the committee. In addition, the others felt that since Alice had never met the Lovells, the time spent alone with them at the church would give her an opportunity to become acquainted with them.

The affection and pride the Larchers had in the old, stately, well-preserved structure that is the First Baptist Church of Cedar City was evident in their words and manner as they showed John and Alice Lovell the particular appointments and points of interest in the building. The Lovells could not help but be impressed. John had not expected the sanctuary to be so spacious. He tested the acoustics and found that they were excellent. Alice gave particular attention to the educational building and was delighted with the charm of the children's rooms. Only the necessity of meeting the rest of the committee for dinner kept them from lingering a much longer time.

Dinner was at the country club. The last such affair with the Benders, which had been held in a home, had resulted in a considerable amount of work for the women. By eating at the country club, it was hoped that everyone, not only the pulpit committee members but their husbands and wives, would have ample opportunity to converse with the Lovells. This proved to be true.

The meal was pleasant and relaxing. After eating, the group returned to the Airds' home to spend the evening. There they gathered in the living room to talk. Strangely enough, they never did get around to a formal interview. In what seemed like a very short time, the evening had passed, and Alice and John Lovell were saying good-night.

As had been previously agreed, the pulpit committee went into a business meeting as soon as the Lovells left. They met upstairs in the den while the others continued to visit in the living room. It was almost midnight when the meeting started. Gil Frazer had gone to drive the Lovells back to the motel. Dorothy served coffee to those who were left. She decided not to take coffee up to the others, not wanting to disturb their meeting. In a few minutes they would be back down. She would keep the pot perking.

When Gil Frazer returned thirty minutes later, the meeting was still going on.

"What are they doing up there?" he asked.

"I guess they're finding when they get down to it, that deciding on a minister is a difficult job."

"I thought they had made up their minds before inviting Pastor John to Cedar City," said Gil.

Dorothy involuntarily glanced up the stairs to the closed door at the top. She, too, couldn't help wondering about the delay. But it was a big decision and not one that any one of the five would take lightly. However, it was getting very late. They had all looked tired when they went into the meeting. She wondered if perhaps they might not have been wiser to get a night's rest and make their decision in the morning. While she was still mulling all this over in her mind, the door at the top of the stairs opened.

They came down to the living room strangely quiet. It was Dick Walker who finally spoke.

"Well, we've got ourselves a minister – that is, if he wants us." His voice sounded flat.

Strangely, this was not how she thought it would be. Even discounting for the late hour and for the tiring strain of the long evening, she had expected that when they finally came to a decision, it would be a moment of celebration and enthusiasm. Not like this. When the last of the couples had left, she turned to Jack and asked how it had gone.

He shook his head and said wryly, "I guess we felt very much like a bridegroom just before he is to say, 'I do!' "

"And how," she asked, "does a bridegroom feel just before he says, 'I do'?"

Aird laughed and tousled her hair. "Come on, let's go to bed."

The next morning, the Lovells were given a tour of the city. Following this, Walt Bosch and Aird met with John Lovell to discuss financial matters.

They met in the pastor's office. Walt motioned for John to sit at the desk, but he declined and eased himself into an upright chair in the corner of the room. Aird smiled, not at John Lovell's pointed refusal to sit at the pastor's desk, but rather because the chair he did sit in was the one most often used by Dr. Post on those occasions when he had attended the board of trustees' meetings held in his office.

The poise and self-assurance that had marked John Lovell when Aird first met him was no less apparent now as he discussed his salary requirements. The strength and vitality of the man seemed to burst forth in every word he spoke.

"I'm aware, of course," he was saying, "from reading your operating budget that you have been paying and are budgeted for considerably less than I would feel to be adequate. I can assure you that my major consideration is not monetary — that's obvious or I would have found a more lucrative field." There was that infectious laugh again. "But I strongly believe that a church congregation should stand up to its financial responsibilities and not ask its minister to bear a financial burden because of its own shortcomings."

Aird exchanged glances with Walt and wondered if he was thinking also of the trustees' meeting hardly a year ago when Frank Post had sat in that same chair where John Lovell now sat. He had sat there, his small frame hunched forward, his eyes almost closed, and had listened to Walt Bosch present a salary study for an assistant minister which showed that the amount needed to obtain a qualified man for that position would require a salary figure embarrassingly close to what was being paid Dr. Post as senior minister. Then Frank

Post, in characteristic style, had touched the heart of the problem.

"Well, you see, this report tells you only what you already knew or at least strongly suspected." He had spoken slowly and his eyes had closed even more. "If you want to get a well-qualified young man, it's going to cost money. I don't think you should worry too much about the disparity between his and my own salary. You'd better pay the price." He had opened his eyes and adjusted his glasses on his nose. "Of course, someday it will be necessary for you to face head-on the salary inequity that exists. The $7200 you pay me is hard to wring out of the budget now, but someday – and it isn't too far off, considering my age – you will be looking for a new minister. It's going to come as a rude shock to some of you that you won't get a man of the caliber you need for the salary that is now paid. Some adjustment will have to be made."

They had known he was right, and more than one on the board vowed right then to face up to this gross injustice and urge the membership to correct this salary inequity at the next annual church meeting. Unfortunately, like so many vows, it was made too late.

Walt offered John the salary figure that the trustees had agreed to offer. It was accepted. So likewise were the ministerial expense allowances. Next the discussion turned to housing. Walt explained that a membership meeting would be held the very next night for the purpose of getting approval to sell the parsonage and build a new home suitable to the future minister's needs. There was no doubt, Walt assured him, that the congregation would approve the proposal. This seemed to cover the last possible problem area of discussion, and Aird looked at Lovell for some sign of agreement. Lovell was obviously distressed.

"Is there something wrong?"

"You speak about a new parsonage," he answered. "Have you considered just offering a housing allowance and letting your minister purchase his own home?"

Aird told him that this had been considered, but not seriously. It was the feeling of the pulpit committee that the church membership would not accept such a proposal.

The frown hadn't left his face. "Alice and I feel strongly that we should have our own home and not depend on its being furnished by the church."

"Why do you feel this way?" asked Walt.

It was a direct question, and it received a direct and impassioned answer. Although Lovell's logic was irrefutable, they were just not authorized to agree to such a request. Aird asked him to consider the offer made. John said he would talk it over with Alice and reply by letter the next day. They shook hands and said good-bye. As they watched him leave, Walt prophesied to Aird, "He would make a great minister for us, but we have lost him on the housing issue." Aird, heavy-heartedly, agreed. It looked as though they had struck out again.

eighteen

THERE ARE SOME THINGS that can't be explained – they just happen. What took place at the church business meeting fell into that category. Certainly nothing in the planning gave any promise of what was to happen. When Hal Larcher, the moderator, had called the meeting three weeks before, he had done so for the express purpose of obtaining membership approval to sell the parsonage, and nothing more. This in itself presented some problems because of the sentimental attachment so many of the congregation had for the old house. But to do away with a parsonage altogether! That was more than the moderator was prepared to ask. Yet, this was precisely what was required to bring John and Alice Lovell to Jackson.

Aird sat leaden-hearted listening to the meeting drone on to its inevitable conclusion: the presentation of the proposal, the arguments pro, the arguments con, and finally, the decision to go along with the recommendation of the trustees. The meeting was held in the sanctuary. Dorothy and he were sitting halfway back in the middle section. The Bosches were sitting in their regular Sunday morning seats down near the front in the far left section. Aird wondered if Walt, too, was hearing once again Lovell's impassioned speech on why he should own his own home. If the interview with him yesterday had made clear any one thing, it was that the action being taken here tonight would be of no avail as far as bringing the Lovells to Cedar City. They could write him off as lost.

And then it happened! Hal Larcher asked if there were any questions from the floor before the motion authorizing the board of trustees to sell the old parsonage and search out a new one was voted upon. Ken Peters stood up.

"I have a question. Has any thought been given to the possibility of allowing the new minister – whoever he happens to be – to have a housing allowance and furnish his own home?"

Was it a casual question thrown out merely as a matter of curiosity? Did he have an inkling that the committee was considering a candidate and this was a vital issue? Aird didn't know, but whatever the reason for Ken's question, it was the voice of rekindled hope. He glanced over quickly at Walt Bosch. He had half turned around in his pew and was looking back toward Peters, who was standing just a few rows behind Aird. He knew the significance of this question for the candidacy of Lovell. Would he speak now to keep the question open? He sat still as did Aird. It would be up to the moderator to either let the question die with a generalized or nondescript answer, or allow open discussion. Aird waited tensely for Hal Larcher to indicate how the question would be answered.

"Ken Peters has asked the question, 'Have we given

any thought to providing our next minister with a housing allowance instead of furnishing a parsonage?' " After he had repeated the question, Hal stood there for a moment saying nothing while his hand fumbled with the mike on the lectern before him. When he spoke, it was clear that he had decided to give the question full treatment.

"I know," he said, "that the pulpit committee has had some thought on this matter. Perhaps the chairman of that committee would like to answer the question." Aird silently blessed the moderator and stood up.

"Until recently no thought was given to the idea of our minister owning his own home. However, there are a number of reasons why he should, some of which became painfully evident with the death of our pastor, Dr. Post." He glanced around – Norma Post was sitting in the rear of the sanctuary. He wished she weren't there to hear what he was about to say, but there was no turning back now.

"The sudden death of a minister places a heavy burden on his family under any condition. The opportunity to save on a minister's salary is negligible. The insurance and pension benefits are minimal. Also, for the family to be placed in the position of having to move out of their home to make room for a new minister can be a harrowing experience, both emotionally and economically. In the present situation in our church, Mrs. Post and her daughter have moved into an apartment. Although no pressure was applied by the church, Mrs. Post was painfully aware right from the moment of the loss of our pastor that she was living in someone else's home and would be required to leave. No minister should be expected to place his family in such a position. There is a limit to what a minister must give in the name of commitment. But this is only one aspect of the question. If a minister reaches retirement age after spending a lifetime in church-furnished parsonages, he finds that for the first time he must provide his own home. He must do this out of whatever savings and pension he has. The financial problem is further compounded because he can be assured that the price of the home he buys will be inflated far beyond the original value of whatever money he has saved. The only way a minister can hope to have a suitable retirement home without an unreasonable financial burden is to be a property owner when he is young so that his property can appreciate through the years leading up to retirement. But as important as these reasons are, there is another reason for a minister owning his own home that is equally compelling. There are many local issues that come up that require a vote of property owners only. One example would be a tax millage for the school district. A minister who lives in a church-furnished parsonage is disfranchised when such an election comes up. Often our own Dr. Post spoke from the pulpit about the concern of the church on certain local issues; and even while he urged all of us to get out and vote, he himself could not. Our minister should not be forced into that sort of situation. To specifically answer Ken's question: Until the present time the pulpit committee has not requested that consideration be given to allowing our minister to own his own home by providing a housing allowance, but the question is pertinent and I see no reason why it cannot be considered here today by the church body."

As he sat down, Jim Fuller, one of the trustees, arose.

"This question opens some interesting possibilities. The idea of a minister owning his own home has gained quite a bit of credence in the last couple of years. I certainly think that it should be considered carefully in this instance. Of major importance are the tax angles. But in principle I must say I endorse the idea."

The door was open. The next fifteen minutes brought several more members to their feet for a point of view on the issue. When it had been talked out, the congregation voted with but one dissenting vote to authorize the trustees to sell the parsonage and allow the pulpit committee to stipulate a housing allowance with an acceptable candidate if this should appear feasible.

Aird drove home elated. It wasn't until he wheeled his car into the driveway that he was aware that Dorothy, rather than sharing his elation, was unusually subdued. He asked her why.

"It's Norma Post. I wish she hadn't been there to hear all the talk about the parsonage."

"She was there because she wanted to be."

"I know. She wants to show an interest, but, nevertheless, it must have hurt her to hear the things that were said about the parsonage."

"She knows its inadequacies probably better than anyone else."

"Even so, she raised a family in that house. She lived there for more than sixteen years. She, no doubt, has many fond memories. I'll bet it didn't seem as rundown to her as you painted it today. Besides, what do you think her thoughts must have been when you sold the idea of a housing allowance for the next minister? How about Dr. Post — didn't he deserve the same consideration?"

"You're right, and I guess Norma might find good cause to feel pained, but we can't do anything now about the past. We can make sure, though, that the next man is not asked to sacrifice as much. Come on. Let's go in the house. I want to call Lovell and let him know about our change in thinking on the parsonage before he turns us down."

It was Alice who answered the phone. "Oh, hello, Jack. Here, I'll let you speak to John."

"Hello, Pastor John here," he answered.

The same warmth, but his voice was subdued.

"Jack, Alice and I have thought of nothing since we saw you last but your church and the offer made to me by your pulpit committee. This morning I wrote you a letter. . . ."

"Wait a minute," Aird interrupted, "don't even tell me what you wrote until I tell you about the meeting held tonight. I told you previously that it was called to consider selling the parsonage. Well, before it was over, the membership also agreed to allow the new minister to have a housing allowance in lieu of a parsonage if he so wished."

Aird thought he heard a long drawn-out sigh at the other end of the line. When John finally spoke, his voice was charged with emotion. "Alice and I both felt that we were particularly called to the church in Cedar City, and yet we also felt that we couldn't, in good conscience, take another assignment which wouldn't offer us the possibility to provide a home of our own for our family. Jack, the letter I wrote you and which is now in the mail turns down your call. When it arrives, just ignore it. On the basis of what you have just told me, I'll get another letter off to you today."

"You will come?"

"Yes, on the basis of what you have just told me, Alice and I accept your call—and, Jack, we won't let your church down. We will put everything we have into the ministry of your church."

Aird put down the receiver. The search was over. Somehow he felt almost unreal. There was an emptiness—a lightness. It was as though a part of him, a burdensome part of him, had disintegrated—like a boy getting out of his long johns at the first blush of spring. He turned to Dorothy who had been sitting nearby while he telephoned. "He's coming! We don't have to look anymore!"

She was still thinking of Norma Post. "You know, I think every minister we interviewed asked questions about Dr. Post's widow and expressed, it seemed to me, some sort of concern about her being in the church—except John Lovell. He never talked about it at all. I think he will welcome her presence—really, truly, be happy that she is there."

Aird prayed she was right.

nineteen

JUNE FIFTH WAS ALSO AIRD'S SISTER'S BIRTHDAY. He thought of that as he and Pastor John followed the choir from the rear of the sanctuary to the chancel. The congregation was singing. So was the choir. But Pastor John's voice could be heard distinctly from the rest. Aird glanced his way. He made an imposing figure in his ministerial robe. Was there a hint in his face of uneasiness? There need not be. The committee had done its homework well in preparing for this significant day in their church.

From the moment it had been decided that the candidate would conduct a Sunday morning service prior to the membership vote on his acceptance, the committee had prepared for the occasion. The tape recordings of his sermons were played to the board of deacons and the board of Christian education. Dick, Marion, and Alice spoke to all the adult church school classes giving biographical sketches of the Lovell family and answering any questions that anyone might have. A letter was sent to every member of the church announcing Lovell's anticipated visit and once again giving a biographical description on the unlikely possibility that there were some yet unaware of his identity.

Seated now in the chancel looking out over the congregation, Aird looked at faces he had not seen in many months. The main floor of the sanctuary appeared to be filled and the balcony had few empty seats. Aird sensed a feeling of expectancy as he introduced Pastor John. But the feeling was more than expectancy. It was an awkwardness – a self-consciousness – not only on the part of the congregation, but on Pastor John's part, too. It was in the ring of his voice, in the nervous twitter of the congregation in reaction to a humorous remark. The feeling was like a meeting of two people for the first time who knew that they were expected to become friends, who wanted to become friends, who jolly well believed that when all the formalities were over that they would become friends.

Not until the reception following the service did the John Lovell the pulpit committee had met in Illinois emerge. Standing with his wife Alice by his side, and flanked by Dick Walker and Marion Frazer, he managed to meet just about everyone who had been present at the worship service. Now his genuine warmth and friendliness were back at work. The introductions, rather than being mere formalities, were animated snatches of conversation. When he had shaken the hand of the last person in line, he had matched enough faces with names to enable him to mingle with the group during refreshments and call many by name. Alice, too, was introducing the Cedar City people to her ready wit and easy conversation. And this staid, conservative midwestern church group appeared to be eating it up. That same evening the congregation met to vote on the committee's recommendation. It was a formality. The vote was unanimous to call John Lovell to the First Baptist Church of Cedar City.

Everyone was there. Hal Larcher, the church moderator, conducted the service. Dr. Worden, the State Executive Secretary, read the charge to the incoming minister. Rev. Earl Patton gave the sermon. Seated in the congregation giving moral support to this new colleague in their midst were many of the ministers of Cedar City and the surrounding area. In the front center pew sat Alice Lovell, her mother, and the two children, Philip and Sharon.

Aird could see all of them from where he sat in the back with Dorothy. But his eyes were mainly on Pastor John. What was there about this man? He had arrived in Cedar City just two weeks ago. Already something mysterious, something magical, was taking place. This church that but two years ago had celebrated its 125th anniversary was once again young. There was laughter and goodwill, zeal and concern, love and fellowship.

This day, this installation service, marked the official demise of the pulpit committee, but really the committee had already melted away.

The committee members who had worked with him had quietly and effortlessly taken up their normal church life and responsibilities where they had left off twelve months before.

Aird, too, had eased back into the mainstream of the church body, but still one thing bugged him. How had this thing happened? After searching for so long and so hard, suddenly it had seemed that this man was there. Was his presence really a result of their search, or in some way did God truly provide? It was not a thought he would want to discuss at his conference table on a Monday morning.

When the service was over, there was a current of traffic down to the front of the sanctuary where Pastor John, flanked by the lay leaders of the church, was standing to receive the good wishes of his people.

Aird and his wife stood for a moment and watched the scene. Finally, he turned to her and smiled.

"What is it?"

"It's all over," he said.

"You mean no more meetings – no more trips? Our weekends are free? There will be time for screens, lawns, and leaky faucets?"

"Yes. . . . Well. . . ."

"What do you mean, well?"

"I think I'll write a book!"